Avant-Garde
AI
Driverless Cars

Practical Advances in
Artificial Intelligence and Machine Learning

Dr. Lance B. Eliot, MBA, PhD

DEDICATION

To my incredible son, Michael, and my incredible daughter, Lauren.

Forest fortuna adiuvat (from the Latin; good fortune favors the brave).

CONTENTS

Lance B. Eliot

ACKNOWLEDGMENTS

I have been the beneficiary of advice and counsel by many friends, colleagues, family, investors, and many others. I want to thank everyone that has aided me throughout my career. I write from the heart and the head, having experienced first-hand what it means to have others around you that support you during the good times and the tough times.

To Warren Bennis, one of my doctoral advisors and ultimately a colleague, I offer my deepest thanks and appreciation, especially for his calm and insightful wisdom and support.

To Mark Stevens and his generous efforts toward funding and supporting the USC Stevens Center for Innovation.

To Lloyd Greif and the USC Lloyd Greif Center for Entrepreneurial Studies for their ongoing encouragement of founders and entrepreneurs.

To Peter Drucker, William Wang, Aaron Levie, Peter Kim, Jon Kraft, Cindy Crawford, Jenny Ming, Steve Milligan, Chis Underwood, Frank Gehry, Buzz Aldrin, Steve Forbes, Bill Thompson, Dave Dillon, Alan Fuerstman, Larry Ellison, Jim Sinegal, John Sperling, Mark Stevenson, Anand Nallathambi, Thomas Barrack, Jr., and many other innovators and leaders that I have met and gained mightily from doing so.

Thanks to Ed Trainor, Kevin Anderson, James Hickey, Wendell Jones, Ken Harris, DuWayne Peterson, Mike Brown, Jim Thornton, Abhi Beniwal, Al Biland, John Nomura, Eliot Weinman, John Desmond, and many others for their unwavering support during my career.

And most of all thanks as always to Michael and Lauren, for their ongoing support and for having seen me writing and heard much of this material during the many months involved in writing it. To their patience and willingness to listen.

INTRODUCTION

This is a book that provides the newest innovations and the latest Artificial Intelligence (AI) advances about the emerging nature of AI-based autonomous self-driving driverless cars. Via recent advances in Artificial Intelligence (AI) and Machine Learning (ML), we are nearing the day when vehicles can control themselves and will not require and nor rely upon human intervention to perform their driving tasks (or, that <u>allow</u> for human intervention, but only *require* human intervention in very limited ways).

Similar to my other related books, which I describe in a moment and list the chapters in the Appendix A of this book, I am particularly focused on those advances that pertain to self-driving cars. The phrase "autonomous vehicles" is often used to refer to any kind of vehicle, whether it is ground-based or in the air or sea, and whether it is a cargo hauling trailer truck or a conventional passenger car. Though the aspects described in this book are certainly applicable to all kinds of autonomous vehicles, I am focused more so here on cars.

Indeed, I am especially known for my role in aiding the advancement of self-driving cars, serving currently as the Executive Director of the Cybernetic Self-Driving Cars Institute.. In addition to writing software, designing and developing systems and software for self-driving cars, I also speak and write quite a bit about the topic. This book is a collection of some of my more advanced essays. For those of you that might have seen my essays posted elsewhere, I have updated them and integrated them into this book as one handy cohesive package.

You might be interested in companion books that I have written that provide additional key innovations and fundamentals about self-driving cars. Those books are entitled **"Introduction to Driverless Self-Driving Cars," "Advances in AI and Autonomous Vehicles: Cybernetic Self-Driving Cars," "Self-Driving Cars: "The Mother of All AI Projects," "Innovation and Thought Leadership on Self-Driving Driverless Cars," "New Advances in AI Autonomous Driverless Self-Driving Cars,"** and **"Autonomous Vehicle Driverless Self-Driving Cars and**

Artificial Intelligence," "Transformative Artificial Intelligence Driverless Self-Driving Cars," "Disruptive Artificial Intelligence and Driverless Self-Driving Cars, and "State-of-the-Art AI Driverless Self-Driving Cars," and "Top Trends in AI Self-Driving Cars," and "AI Innovations and Self-Driving Cars," "Crucial Advances for AI Driverless Cars," "Sociotechnical Insights and AI Driverless Cars," "Pioneering Advances for AI Driverless Cars" and "Leading Edge Trends for AI Driverless Cars," "The Cutting Edge of AI Autonomous Cars" and "The Next Wave of AI Self-Driving Cars" and "Revolutionary Innovations of AI Self-Driving Cars," and "AI Self-Driving Cars Breakthroughs," "Trailblazing Trends for AI Self-Driving Cars," "Ingenious Strides for AI Driverless Cars," "AI Self-Driving Cars Inventiveness," "Visionary Secrets of AI Driverless Cars," "Spearheading AI Self-Driving Cars," "Spurring AI Self-Driving Cars," and "Avant-Garde AI Driverless Cars" (they are all available via Amazon). Appendix A has a listing of the chapters covered in those books.

For the introduction herein to this book, I am going to borrow my introduction from those companion books, since it does a good job of laying out the landscape of self-driving cars and my overall viewpoints on the topic. The remainder of the book is all new material that does not appear in the companion books.

INTRODUCTION TO SELF-DRIVING CARS

This is a book about self-driving cars. Someday in the future, we'll all have self-driving cars and this book will perhaps seem antiquated, but right now, we are at the forefront of the self-driving car wave. Daily news bombards us with flashes of new announcements by one car maker or another and leaves the impression that within the next few weeks or maybe months that the self-driving car will be here. A casual non-technical reader would assume from these news flashes that in fact we must be on the cusp of a true self-driving car.

Here's a real news flash: We are still quite a distance from having a true self-driving car. It is years to go before we get there.

Why is that? Because a true self-driving car is akin to a moonshot. In the same manner that getting us to the moon was an incredible feat, likewise is achieving a true self-driving car. Anybody that suggests or even brashly states that the true self-driving car is nearly here should be viewed with great skepticism. Indeed, you'll see that I often tend to use the word "hogwash" or "crock" when I assess much of the decidedly *fake news* about self-driving cars. Those of us on the inside know that what is often reported to the outside is malarkey. Few of the insiders are willing to say so. I have no such hesitation.

Indeed, I've been writing a popular blog post about self-driving cars and hitting hard on those that try to wave their hands and pretend that we are on the imminent verge of true self-driving cars. For many years, I've been known as the AI Insider. Besides writing about AI, I also develop AI software. I do what I describe. It also gives me insights into what others that are doing AI are really doing versus what it is said they are doing.

Many faithful readers had asked me to pull together my insightful short essays and put them into another book, which you are now holding.

For those of you that have been reading my essays over the years, this collection not only puts them together into one handy package, I also updated the essays and added new material. For those of you that are new to the topic of self-driving cars and AI, I hope you find these essays approachable and informative. I also tend to have a writing style with a bit of a voice, and so you'll see that I am times have a wry sense of humor and poke at conformity.

As a former professor and founder of an AI research lab, I for many years wrote in the formal language of academic writing. I published in referred journals and served as an editor for several AI journals. This writing here is not of the nature, and I have adopted a different and more informal style for these essays. That being said, I also do mention from time-to-time more rigorous material on AI and encourage you all to dig into those deeper and more formal materials if so interested.

I am also an AI practitioner. This means that I write AI software for a living. Currently, I head-up the Cybernetics Self-Driving Car Institute, where we are developing AI software for self-driving cars. I am excited to also report that my son, also a software engineer, heads-up our Cybernetics Self-Driving Car Lab. What I have helped to start, and for which he is an integral part, ultimately he will carry long into the future after I have retired. My daughter, a marketing whiz, also is integral to our efforts as head of our Marketing group. She too will carry forward the legacy now being formulated.

For those of you that are reading this book and have a penchant for writing code, you might consider taking a look at the open source code available for self-driving cars. This is a handy place to start learning how to develop AI for self-driving cars. There are also many new educational courses spring forth. There is a growing body of those wanting to learn about and develop self-driving cars, and a growing body of colleges, labs, and other avenues by which you can learn about self-driving cars.

This book will provide a foundation of aspects that I think will get you ready for those kinds of more advanced training opportunities. If you've already taken those classes, you'll likely find these essays especially interesting as they offer a perspective that I am betting few other instructors or faculty offered to you. These are challenging essays that ask you to think beyond the conventional about self-driving cars.

THE MOTHER OF ALL AI PROJECTS

In June 2017, Apple CEO Tim Cook came out and finally admitted that Apple has been working on a self-driving car. As you'll see in my essays, Apple was enmeshed in secrecy about their self-driving car efforts. We have only been able to read the tea leaves and guess at what Apple has been up to. The notion of an iCar has been floating for quite a while, and self-driving engineers and researchers have been signing tight-lipped Non-Disclosure Agreements (NDA's) to work on projects at Apple that were as shrouded in mystery as any military invasion plans might be.

Tim Cook said something that many others in the Artificial Intelligence (AI) field have been saying, namely, the creation of a self-driving car has got to be the mother of all AI projects. In other words, it is in fact a tremendous moonshot for AI. If a self-driving car can be crafted and the AI works as we hope, it means that we have made incredible strides with AI and that therefore it opens many other worlds of potential breakthrough accomplishments that AI can solve.

Is this hyperbole? Am I just trying to make AI seem like a miracle worker and so provide self-aggrandizing statements for those of us writing the AI software for self-driving cars? No, it is not hyperbole. Developing a true self-driving car is really, really, really hard to do. Let me take a moment to explain why. As a side note, I realize that the Apple CEO is known for at times uttering hyperbole, and he had previously said for example that the year 2012 was "the mother of all years," and he had said that the release of iOS 10 was "the mother of all releases" – all of which does suggest he likes to use the handy "mother of" expression. But, I assure you, in terms of true self-driving cars, he has hit the nail on the head. For sure.

When you think about a moonshot and how we got to the moon, there are some identifiable characteristics and those same aspects can be applied to creating a true self-driving car. You'll notice that I keep putting the word "true" in front of the self-driving car expression. I do so because as per my essay about the various levels of self-driving cars, there are some self-driving cars that are only somewhat of a self-driving car. The somewhat versions are ones that require a human driver to be ready to intervene. In my view, that's not a true self-driving car. A true self-driving car is one that requires no human driver intervention at all. It is a car that can entirely undertake via automation the driving task without any human driver needed. This is the essence of what is known as a Level 5 self-driving car. We are currently at the Level 2 and Level 3 mark, and not yet at Level 5.

Getting to the moon involved aspects such as having big stretch goals, incremental progress, experimentation, innovation, and so on. Let's review how this applied to the moonshot of the bygone era, and how it applies to the self-driving car moonshot of today.

Big Stretch Goal

Trying to take a human and deliver the human to the moon, and bring them back, safely, was an extremely large stretch goal at the time. No one knew whether it could be done. The technology wasn't available yet. The cost was huge. The determination would need to be fierce. Etc. To reach a Level 5 self-driving car is going to be the same. It is a big stretch goal. We can readily get to the Level 3, and we are able to see the Level 4 just up ahead, but a Level 5 is still an unknown as to if it is doable. It should eventually be doable and in the same way that we thought we'd eventually get to the moon, but when it will occur is a different story.

Incremental Progress

Getting to the moon did not happen overnight in one fell swoop. It took years and years of incremental progress to get there. Likewise for self-driving cars. Google has famously been striving to get to the Level 5, and pretty much been willing to forgo dealing with the intervening levels, but most of the other self-driving car makers are doing the incremental route. Let's get a good Level 2 and a somewhat Level 3 going. Then, let's improve the Level 3 and get a somewhat Level 4 going. Then, let's improve the Level 4 and finally arrive at a Level 5. This seems to be the prevalent way that we are going to achieve the true self-driving car.

Experimentation

You likely know that there were various experiments involved in perfecting the approach and technology to get to the moon. As per making incremental progress, we first tried to see if we could get a rocket to go into space and safety return, then put a monkey in there, then with a human, then we went all the way to the moon but didn't land, and finally we arrived at the mission that actually landed on the moon. Self-driving cars are the same way. We are doing simulations of self-driving cars. We do testing of self-driving cars on private land under controlled situations. We do testing of self-driving cars on public roadways, often having to meet regulatory requirements including for example having an engineer or equivalent in the car to take over the controls if needed. And so on. Experiments big and small are needed to figure out what works and what doesn't.

Innovation

There are already some advances in AI that are allowing us to progress toward self-driving cars. We are going to need even more advances. Innovation in all aspects of technology are going to be required to achieve a true self-driving car. By no means do we already have everything in-hand that we need to get there. Expect new inventions and new approaches, new algorithms, etc.

Setbacks

Most of the pundits are avoiding talking about potential setbacks in the progress toward self-driving cars. Getting to the moon involved many setbacks, some of which you never have heard of and were buried at the time so as to not dampen enthusiasm and funding for getting to the moon. A recurring theme in many of my included essays is that there are going to be setbacks as we try to arrive at a true self-driving car. Take a deep breath and be ready. I just hope the setbacks don't completely stop progress. I am sure that it will cause progress to alter in a manner that we've not yet seen in the self-driving car field. I liken the self-driving car of today to the excitement everyone had for Uber when it first got going. Today, we have a different view of Uber and with each passing day there are more regulations to the ride sharing business and more concerns raised. The darling child only stays a darling until finally that child acts up. It will happen the same with self-driving cars.

SELF-DRIVING CARS CHALLENGES

But what exactly makes things so hard to have a true self-driving car, you might be asking. You have seen cruise control for years and years. You've lately seen cars that can do parallel parking. You've seen YouTube videos of Tesla drivers that put their hands out the window as their car zooms along the highway, and seen to therefore be in a self-driving car. Aren't we just needing to put a few more sensors onto a car and then we'll have in-hand a true self-driving car? Nope.

Consider for a moment the nature of the driving task. We don't just let anyone at any age drive a car. Worldwide, most countries won't license a driver until the age of 18, though many do allow a learner's permit at the age of 15 or 16. Some suggest that a younger age would be physically too small to reach the controls of the car. Though this might be the case, we could easily adjust the controls to allow for younger aged and thus smaller stature. It's not their physical size that matters. It's their cognitive development that matters.

To drive a car, you need to be able to reason about the car, what the car can and cannot do. You need to know how to operate the car. You need to know about how other cars on the road drive. You need to know what is allowed in driving such as speed limits and driving within marked lanes. You need to be able to react to situations and be able to avoid getting into accidents. You need to ascertain when to hit your brakes, when to steer clear of a pedestrian, and how to keep from ramming that motorcyclist that just cut you off.

Many of us had taken courses on driving. We studied about driving and took driver training. We had to take a test and pass it to be able to drive. The point being that though most adults take the driving task for granted, and we often "mindlessly" drive our cars, there is a significant amount of cognitive effort that goes into driving a car. After a while, it becomes second nature. You don't especially think about how you drive, you just do it. But, if you watch a novice driver, say a teenager learning to drive, you suddenly realize that there is a lot more complexity to it than we seem to realize.

Furthermore, driving is a very serious task. I recall when my daughter and son first learned to drive. They are both very conscientious people. They wanted to make sure that whatever they did, they did well, and that they did not harm anyone. Every day, when you get into a car, it is probably around 4,000 pounds of hefty metal and plastics (about two tons), and it is a lethal weapon. Think about it. You drive down the street in an object that weighs two tons and with the engine it can accelerate and ram into anything you want to hit. The damage a car can inflict is very scary. Both my children were surprised that they were being given the right to maneuver this monster of a beast that could cause tremendous harm entirely by merely letting go of the steering wheel for a moment or taking your eyes off the road.

In fact, in the United States alone there are about 30,000 deaths per year by auto accidents, which is around 100 per day. Given that there are about 263 million cars in the United States, I am actually more amazed that the number of fatalities is not a lot higher. During my morning commute, I look at all the thousands of cars on the freeway around me, and I think that if all of them decided to go zombie and drive in a crazy maniac way, there would be many people dead. Somehow, incredibly, each day, most people drive relatively safely. To me, that's a miracle right there. Getting millions and millions of people to be safe and sane when behind the wheel of a two ton mobile object, it's a feat that we as a society should admire with pride.

So, hopefully you are in agreement that the driving task requires a great deal of cognition. You don't' need to be especially smart to drive a car, and we've done quite a bit to make car driving viable for even the average dolt. There isn't an IQ test that you need to take to drive a car. If you can read and write, and pass a test, you pretty much can legally drive a car. There are of course some that drive a car and are not legally permitted to do so, plus there are private areas such as farms where drivers are young, but for public roadways in the United States, you can be generally of average intelligence (or less) and be able to legally drive.

This though makes it seem like the cognitive effort must not be much. If the cognitive effort was truly hard, wouldn't we only have Einstein's that could drive a car? We have made sure to keep the driving task as simple as we can, by making the controls easy and relatively standardized, and by having roads that are relatively standardized, and so on. It is as though Disneyland has put their Autopia into the real-world, by us all as a society agreeing that roads will be a certain way, and we'll all abide by the various rules of driving.

A modest cognitive task by a human is still something that stymies AI. You certainly know that AI has been able to beat chess players and be good at other kinds of games. This type of narrow cognition is not what car driving is about. Car driving is much wider. It requires knowledge about the world, which a chess playing AI system does not need to know. The cognitive aspects of driving are on the one hand seemingly simple, but at the same time require layer upon layer of knowledge about cars, people, roads, rules, and a myriad of other "common sense" aspects. We don't have any AI systems today that have that same kind of breadth and depth of awareness and knowledge.

As revealed in my essays, the self-driving car of today is using trickery to do particular tasks. It is all very narrow in operation. Plus, it currently assumes that a human driver is ready to intervene. It is like a child that we have taught to stack blocks, but we are needed to be right there in case the child stacks them too high and they begin to fall over. AI of today is brittle, it is narrow, and it does not approach the cognitive abilities of humans. This is why the true self-driving car is somewhere out in the future.

Another aspect to the driving task is that it is not solely a mind exercise. You do need to use your senses to drive. You use your eyes a vision sensors to see the road ahead. You vision capability is like a streaming video, which your brain needs to continually analyze as you drive. Where is the road? Is there a pedestrian in the way? Is there another car ahead of you? Your senses are relying a flood of info to your brain. Self-driving cars are trying to do the same, by using cameras, radar, ultrasound, and lasers. This is an attempt at mimicking how humans have senses and sensory apparatus.

Thus, the driving task is mental and physical. You use your senses, you use your arms and legs to manipulate the controls of the car, and you use your brain to assess the sensory info and direct your limbs to act upon the controls of the car. This all happens instantly. If you've ever perhaps gotten something in your eye and only had one eye available to drive with, you suddenly realize how dependent upon vision you are. If you have a broken foot with a cast, you suddenly realize how hard it is to control the brake pedal and the accelerator. If you've taken medication and your brain is maybe sluggish, you suddenly realize how much mental strain is required to drive a car.

An AI system that plays chess only needs to be focused on playing chess. The physical aspects aren't important because usually a human moves the chess pieces or the chessboard is shown on an electronic display. Using AI for a more life-and-death task such as analyzing MRI images of patients, this again does not require physical capabilities and instead is done by examining images of bits.

Driving a car is a true life-and-death task. It is a use of AI that can easily and at any moment produce death. For those colleagues of mine that are developing this AI, as am I, we need to keep in mind the somber aspects of this. We are producing software that will have in its virtual hands the lives of the occupants of the car, and the lives of those in other nearby cars, and the lives of nearby pedestrians, etc. Chess is not usually a life-or-death matter.

Driving is all around us. Cars are everywhere. Most of today's AI applications involve only a small number of people. Or, they are behind the scenes and we as humans have other recourse if the AI messes up. AI that is driving a car at 80 miles per hour on a highway had better not mess up. The consequences are grave. Multiply this by the number of cars, if we could put magically self-driving into every car in the USA, we'd have AI running in the 263 million cars. That's a lot of AI spread around. This is AI on a massive scale that we are not doing today and that offers both promise and potential peril.

There are some that want AI for self-driving cars because they envision a world without any car accidents. They envision a world in which there is no car congestion and all cars cooperate with each other. These are wonderful utopian visions.

They are also very misleading. The adoption of self-driving cars is going to be incremental and not overnight. We cannot economically just junk all existing cars. Nor are we going to be able to affordably retrofit existing cars. It is more likely that self-driving cars will be built into new cars and that over many years of gradual replacement of existing cars that we'll see the mix of self-driving cars become substantial in the real-world.

In these essays, I have tried to offer technological insights without being overly technical in my description, and also blended the business, societal, and economic aspects too. Technologists need to consider the non-technological impacts of what they do. Non-technologists should be aware of what is being developed.

We all need to work together to collectively be prepared for the enormous disruption and transformative aspects of true self-driving cars. We all need to be involved in this mother of all AI projects.

WHAT THIS BOOK PROVIDES

What does this book provide to you? It introduces many of the key elements about self-driving cars and does so with an AI based perspective. I weave together technical and non-technical aspects, readily going from being concerned about the cognitive capabilities of the driving task and how the technology is embodying this into self-driving cars, and in the next breath I discuss the societal and economic aspects.

They are all intertwined because that's the way reality is. You cannot separate out the technology per se, and instead must consider it within the milieu of what is being invented and innovated, and do so with a mindset towards the contemporary mores and culture that shape what we are doing and what we hope to do.

WHY THIS BOOK

I wrote this book to try and bring to the public view many aspects about self-driving cars that nobody seems to be discussing.

For business leaders that are either involved in making self-driving cars or that are going to leverage self-driving cars, I hope that this book will enlighten you as to the risks involved and ways in which you should be strategizing about how to deal with those risks.

For entrepreneurs, startups and other businesses that want to enter into the self-driving car market that is emerging, I hope this book sparks your interest in doing so, and provides some sense of what might be prudent to pursue.

For researchers that study self-driving cars, I hope this book spurs your interest in the risks and safety issues of self-driving cars, and also nudges you toward conducting research on those aspects.

For students in computer science or related disciplines, I hope this book will provide you with interesting and new ideas and material, for which you might conduct research or provide some career direction insights for you.

For AI companies and high-tech companies pursuing self-driving cars, this book will hopefully broaden your view beyond just the mere coding and development needed to make self-driving cars.

For all readers, I hope that you will find the material in this book to be stimulating. Some of it will be repetitive of things you already know. But I am pretty sure that you'll also find various eureka moments whereby you'll discover a new technique or approach that you had not earlier thought of. I am also betting that there will be material that forces you to rethink some of your current practices.

I am not saying you will suddenly have an epiphany and change what you are doing. I do think though that you will reconsider or perhaps revisit what you are doing.

For anyone choosing to use this book for teaching purposes, please take a look at my suggestions for doing so, as described in the Appendix. I have found the material handy in courses that I have taught, and likewise other faculty have told me that they have found the material handy, in some cases as extended readings and in other instances as a core part of their course (depending on the nature of the class).

In my writing for this book, I have tried carefully to blend both the practitioner and the academic styles of writing. It is not as dense as is typical academic journal writing, but at the same time offers depth by going into the nuances and trade-offs of various practices.

The word "deep" is in vogue today, meaning getting deeply into a subject or topic, and so is the word "unpack" which means to tease out the underlying aspects of a subject or topic. I have sought to offer material that addresses an issue or topic by going relatively deeply into it and make sure that it is well unpacked.

Finally, in any book about AI, it is difficult to use our everyday words without having some of them be misinterpreted. Specifically, it is easy to anthropomorphize AI. When I say that an AI system "knows" something, I do not want you to construe that the AI system has sentience and "knows" in the same way that humans do. They aren't that way, as yet. I have tried to use quotes around such words from time-to-time to emphasize that the words I am using should not be misinterpreted to ascribe true human intelligence to the AI systems that we know of today. If I used quotes around all such words, the book would be very difficult to read, and so I am doing so judiciously. Please keep that in mind as you read the material, thanks.

COMPANION BOOKS

If you find this material of interest, you might enjoy these too:

1. **"Introduction to Driverless Self-Driving Cars"** by Dr. Lance Eliot

2. **"Innovation and Thought Leadership on Self-Driving Driverless Cars"** by Dr. Lance Eliot

3. **"Advances in AI and Autonomous Vehicles: Cybernetic Self-Driving Cars"** by Dr. Lance Eliot

4. **"Self-Driving Cars: The Mother of All AI Projects"** by Dr. Lance Eliot

5. **"New Advances in AI Autonomous Driverless Self-Driving Cars"** by Dr. Lance Eliot

6. **"Autonomous Vehicle Driverless Self-Driving Cars and Artificial Intelligence"** by Dr. Lance Eliot and Michael B. Eliot

7. **"Transformative Artificial Intelligence Driverless Self-Driving Cars"** by Dr. Lance Eliot

8. **"Disruptive Artificial Intelligence and Driverless Self-Driving Cars"** by Dr. Lance Eliot

9. "State-of-the-Art AI Driverless Self-Driving Cars" by Dr. Lance Eliot

10. **"Top Trends in AI Self-Driving Cars"** by Dr. Lance Eliot

11. **"AI Innovations and Self-Driving Cars"** by Dr. Lance Eliot

12. **"Crucial Advances for AI Driverless Cars"** by Dr. Lance Eliot

13. **"Sociotechnical Insights and AI Driverless Cars"** by Dr. Lance Eliot.

14. **"Pioneering Advances for AI Driverless Cars"** by Dr. Lance Eliot

15. **"Leading Edge Trends for AI Driverless Cars"** by Dr. Lance Eliot

16. **"The Cutting Edge of AI Autonomous Cars"** by Dr. Lance Eliot

17. **"The Next Wave of AI Self-Driving Cars"** by Dr. Lance Eliot

18. **"Revolutionary Innovations of AI Driverless Cars"** by Dr. Lance Eliot

19. **"AI Self-Driving Cars Breakthroughs"** by Dr. Lance Eliot

20. **"Trailblazing Trends for AI Self-Driving Cars"** by Dr. Lance Eliot

21. **"Ingenious Strides for AI Driverless Cars"** by Dr. Lance Eliot

22. **"AI Self-Driving Cars Inventiveness"** by Dr. Lance Eliot

23. **"Visionary Secrets of AI Driverless Cars"** by Dr. Lance Eliot

24. **"Spearheading AI Self-Driving Cars"** by Dr. Lance Eliot

25. **"Spurring AI Self-Driving Cars"** by Dr. Lance Eliot

26. **"Avant-Garde AI Driverless Cars"** by Dr. Lance Eliot

These books are available on Amazon and at other major global booksellers.

CHAPTER 1

ELIOT FRAMEWORK FOR AI SELF-DRIVING CARS

CHAPTER 1

ELIOT FRAMEWORK FOR
AI SELF-DRIVING CARS

This chapter is a core foundational aspect for understanding AI self-driving cars and I have used this same chapter in several of my other books to introduce the reader to essential elements of this field. Once you've read this chapter, you'll be prepared to read the rest of the material since the foundational essence of the components of autonomous AI driverless self-driving cars will have been established for you.

———————

When I give presentations about self-driving cars and teach classes on the topic, I have found it helpful to provide a framework around which the various key elements of self-driving cars can be understood and organized (see diagram at the end of this chapter). The framework needs to be simple enough to convey the overarching elements, but at the same time not so simple that it belies the true complexity of self-driving cars. As such, I am going to describe the framework here and try to offer in a thousand words (or more!) what the framework diagram itself intends to portray.

The core elements on the diagram are numbered for ease of reference. The numbering does not suggest any kind of prioritization of the elements. Each element is crucial. Each element has a purpose, and otherwise would not be included in the framework. For some self-driving cars, a particular element might be more important or somehow distinguished in comparison to other self-driving cars.

You could even use the framework to rate a particular self-driving car, doing so by gauging how well it performs in each of the elements of the framework. I will describe each of the elements, one at a time. After doing so, I'll discuss aspects that illustrate how the elements interact and perform during the overall effort of a self-driving car.

At the Cybernetic Self-Driving Car Institute, we use the framework to keep track of what we are working on, and how we are developing software that fills in what is needed to achieve Level 5 self-driving cars.

D-01: Sensor Capture

Let's start with the one element that often gets the most attention in the press about self-driving cars, namely, the sensory devices for a self-driving car.

On the framework, the box labeled as D-01 indicates "Sensor Capture" and refers to the processes of the self-driving car that involve collecting data from the myriad of sensors that are used for a self-driving car. The types of devices typically involved are listed, such as the use of mono cameras, stereo cameras, LIDAR devices, radar systems, ultrasonic devices, GPS, IMU, and so on.

These devices are tasked with obtaining data about the status of the self-driving car and the world around it. Some of the devices are continually providing updates, while others of the devices await an indication by the self-driving car that the device is supposed to collect data. The data might be first transformed in some fashion by the device itself, or it might instead be fed directly into the sensor capture as raw data. At that point, it might be up to the sensor capture processes to do transformations on the data. This all varies depending upon the nature of the devices being used and how the devices were designed and developed.

D-02: Sensor Fusion

Imagine that your eyeballs receive visual images, your nose receives odors, your ears receive sounds, and in essence each of your distinct sensory devices is getting some form of input. The input befits the nature of the device. Likewise, for a self-driving car, the cameras provide visual images, the radar returns radar reflections, and so on.

Each device provides the data as befits what the device does.

At some point, using the analogy to humans, you need to merge together what your eyes see, what your nose smells, what your ears hear, and piece it all together into a larger sense of what the world is all about and what is happening around you. Sensor fusion is the action of taking the singular aspects from each of the devices and putting them together into a larger puzzle.

Sensor fusion is a tough task. There are some devices that might not be working at the time of the sensor capture. Or, there might some devices that are unable to report well what they have detected. Again, using a human analogy, suppose you are in a dark room and so your eyes cannot see much. At that point, you might need to rely more so on your ears and what you hear. The same is true for a self-driving car. If the cameras are obscured due to snow and sleet, it might be that the radar can provide a greater indication of what the external conditions consist of.

In the case of a self-driving car, there can be a plethora of such sensory devices. Each is reporting what it can. Each might have its difficulties. Each might have its limitations, such as how far ahead it can detect an object. All of these limitations need to be considered during the sensor fusion task.

D-03: Virtual World Model

For humans, we presumably keep in our minds a model of the world around us when we are driving a car. In your mind, you know that the car is going at say 60 miles per hour and that you are on a freeway. You have a model in your mind that your car is surrounded by other cars, and that there are lanes to the freeway. Your model is not only based on what you can see, hear, etc., but also what you know about the nature of the world. You know that at any moment that car ahead of you can smash on its brakes, or the car behind you can ram into your car, or that the truck in the next lane might swerve into your lane.

The AI of the self-driving car needs to have a virtual world model, which it then keeps updated with whatever it is receiving from the sensor fusion, which received its input from the sensor capture and the sensory devices.

D-04: System Action Plan

By having a virtual world model, the AI of the self-driving car is able to keep track of where the car is and what is happening around the car. In addition, the AI needs to determine what to do next. Should the self-driving car hit its brakes? Should the self-driving car stay in its lane or swerve into the lane to the left? Should the self-driving car accelerate or slow down?

A system action plan needs to be prepared by the AI of the self-driving car. The action plan specifies what actions should be taken. The actions need to pertain to the status of the virtual world model. Plus, the actions need to be realizable.

This realizability means that the AI cannot just assert that the self-driving car should suddenly sprout wings and fly. Instead, the AI must be bound by whatever the self-driving car can actually do, such as coming to a halt in a distance of X feet at a speed of Y miles per hour, rather than perhaps asserting that the self-driving car come to a halt in 0 feet as though it could instantaneously come to a stop while it is in motion.

D-05: Controls Activation

The system action plan is implemented by activating the controls of the car to act according to what the plan stipulates. This might mean that the accelerator control is commanded to increase the speed of the car. Or, the steering control is commanded to turn the steering wheel 30 degrees to the left or right.

One question arises as to whether or not the controls respond as they are commanded to do. In other words, suppose the AI has commanded the accelerator to increase, but for some reason it does not do so. Or, maybe it tries to do so, but the speed of the car does not increase. The controls activation feeds back into the virtual world model, and simultaneously the virtual world model is getting updated from the sensors, the sensor capture, and the sensor fusion. This allows the AI to ascertain what has taken place as a result of the controls being commanded to take some kind of action.

By the way, please keep in mind that though the diagram seems to have a linear progression to it, the reality is that these are all aspects of the self-driving car that are happening in parallel and simultaneously. The sensors are capturing data, meanwhile the sensor fusion is taking place, meanwhile the virtual model is being updated, meanwhile the system action plan is being formulated and reformulated, meanwhile the controls are being activated.

This is the same as a human being that is driving a car. They are eyeballing the road, meanwhile they are fusing in their mind the sights, sounds, etc., meanwhile their mind is updating their model of the world around them, meanwhile they are formulating an action plan of what to do, and meanwhile they are pushing their foot onto the pedals and steering the car. In the normal course of driving a car, you are doing all of these at once. I mention this so that when you look at the diagram, you will think of the boxes as processes that are all happening at the same time, and not as though only one happens and then the next.

They are shown diagrammatically in a simplistic manner to help comprehend what is taking place. You though should also realize that they are working in parallel and simultaneous with each other. This is a tough aspect in that the inter-element communications involve latency and other aspects that must be taken into account. There can be delays in one element updating and then sharing its latest status with other elements.

D-06: Automobile & CAN

Contemporary cars use various automotive electronics and a Controller Area Network (CAN) to serve as the components that underlie the driving aspects of a car. There are Electronic Control Units (ECU's) which control subsystems of the car, such as the engine, the brakes, the doors, the windows, and so on.

The elements D-01, D-02, D-03, D-04, D-05 are layered on top of the D-06, and must be aware of the nature of what the D-06 is able to do and not do.

D-07: In-Car Commands

Humans are going to be occupants in self-driving cars. In a Level 5 self-driving car, there must be some form of communication that takes place between the humans and the self-driving car. For example, I go into a self-driving car and tell it that I want to be driven over to Disneyland, and along the way I want to stop at In-and-Out Burger. The self-driving car now parses what I've said and tries to then establish a means to carry out my wishes.

In-car commands can happen at any time during a driving journey. Though my example was about an in-car command when I first got into my self-driving car, it could be that while the self-driving car is carrying out the journey that I change my mind. Perhaps after getting stuck in traffic, I tell the self-driving car to forget about getting the burgers and just head straight over to the theme park. The self-driving car needs to be alert to in-car commands throughout the journey.

D-08: V2X Communications

We will ultimately have self-driving cars communicating with each other, doing so via V2V (Vehicle-to-Vehicle) communications. We will also have self-driving cars that communicate with the roadways and other aspects of the transportation infrastructure, doing so via V2I (Vehicle-to-Infrastructure).

The variety of ways in which a self-driving car will be communicating with other cars and infrastructure is being called V2X, whereby the letter X means whatever else we identify as something that a car should or would want to communicate with. The V2X communications will be taking place simultaneous with everything else on the diagram, and those other elements will need to incorporate whatever it gleans from those V2X communications.

D-09: Deep Learning

The use of Deep Learning permeates all other aspects of the self-driving car. The AI of the self-driving car will be using deep learning to do a better job at the systems action plan, and at the controls activation, and at the sensor fusion, and so on.

Currently, the use of artificial neural networks is the most prevalent form of deep learning. Based on large swaths of data, the neural networks attempt to "learn" from the data and therefore direct the efforts of the self-driving car accordingly.

D-10: Tactical AI

Tactical AI is the element of dealing with the moment-to-moment driving of the self-driving car. Is the self-driving car staying in its lane of the freeway? Is the car responding appropriately to the controls commands? Are the sensory devices working?

For human drivers, the tactical equivalent can be seen when you watch a novice driver such as a teenager that is first driving. They are focused on the mechanics of the driving task, keeping their eye on the road while also trying to properly control the car.

D-11: Strategic AI

The Strategic AI aspects of a self-driving car are dealing with the larger picture of what the self-driving car is trying to do. If I had asked that the self-driving car take me to Disneyland, there is an overall journey map that needs to be kept and maintained.

There is an interaction between the Strategic AI and the Tactical AI. The Strategic AI is wanting to keep on the mission of the driving, while the Tactical AI is focused on the particulars underway in the driving effort. If the Tactical AI seems to wander away from the overarching mission, the Strategic AI wants to see why and get things back on track. If the Tactical AI realizes that there is something amiss on the self-driving car, it needs to alert the Strategic AI accordingly and have an adjustment to the overarching mission that is underway.

D-12: Self-Aware AI

Very few of the self-driving cars being developed are including a Self-Aware AI element, which we at the Cybernetic Self-Driving Car Institute believe is crucial to Level 5 self-driving cars.

The Self-Aware AI element is intended to watch over itself, in the sense that the AI is making sure that the AI is working as intended. Suppose you had a human driving a car, and they were starting to drive erratically. Hopefully, their own self-awareness would make them realize they themselves are driving poorly, such as perhaps starting to fall asleep after having been driving for hours on end. If you had a passenger in the car, they might be able to alert the driver if the driver is starting to do something amiss. This is exactly what the Self-Aware

AI element tries to do, it becomes the overseer of the AI, and tries to detect when the AI has become faulty or confused, and then find ways to overcome the issue.

D-13: Economic

The economic aspects of a self-driving car are not per se a technology aspect of a self-driving car, but the economics do indeed impact the nature of a self-driving car. For example, the cost of outfitting a self-driving car with every kind of possible sensory device is prohibitive, and so choices need to be made about which devices are used. And, for those sensory devices chosen, whether they would have a full set of features or a more limited set of features.

We are going to have self-driving cars that are at the low-end of a consumer cost point, and others at the high-end of a consumer cost point. You cannot expect that the self-driving car at the low-end is going to be as robust as the one at the high-end. I realize that many of the self-driving car pundits are acting as though all self-driving cars will be the same, but they won't be. Just like anything else, we are going to have self-driving cars that have a range of capabilities. Some will be better than others. Some will be safer than others. This is the way of the real-world, and so we need to be thinking about the economics aspects when considering the nature of self-driving cars.

D-14: Societal

This component encompasses the societal aspects of AI which also impacts the technology of self-driving cars. For example, the famous Trolley Problem involves what choices should a self-driving car make when faced with life-and-death matters. If the self-driving car is about to either hit a child standing in the roadway, or instead ram into a tree at the side of the road and possibly kill the humans in the self-driving car, which choice should be made?

We need to keep in mind the societal aspects will underlie the AI of the self-driving car. Whether we are aware of it explicitly or not, the AI will have embedded into it various societal assumptions.

D-15: Innovation

I included the notion of innovation into the framework because we can anticipate that whatever a self-driving car consists of, it will continue to be innovated over time. The self-driving cars coming out in the next several years will undoubtedly be different and less innovative than the versions that come out in ten years hence, and so on.

Framework Overall

For those of you that want to learn about self-driving cars, you can potentially pick a particular element and become specialized in that aspect. Some engineers are focusing on the sensory devices. Some engineers focus on the controls activation. And so on. There are specialties in each of the elements.

Researchers are likewise specializing in various aspects. For example, there are researchers that are using Deep Learning to see how best it can be used for sensor fusion. There are other researchers that are using Deep Learning to derive good System Action Plans. Some are studying how to develop AI for the Strategic aspects of the driving task, while others are focused on the Tactical aspects.

A well-prepared all-around software developer that is involved in self-driving cars should be familiar with all of the elements, at least to the degree that they know what each element does. This is important since whatever piece of the pie that the software developer works on, they need to be knowledgeable about what the other elements are doing.

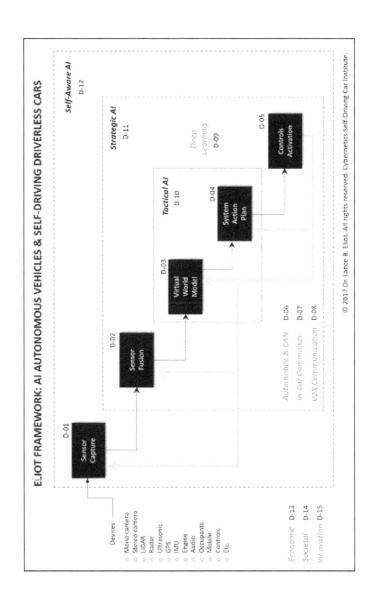

CHAPTER 2

LINEAR NON-THRESHOLD
AND
AI SELF-DRIVING CARS

Lance B. Eliot

CHAPTER 2

LINEAR NON-THRESHOLD
AND AI SELF-DRIVING CARS

The controversial Linear No-Threshold (LNT) graph has been in the news recently.

LNT is a statistical type of model that has been used primarily in health-related areas such as dealing with exposures to radiation and other human-endangering substances such as toxic chemicals.

Essentially, the standard version of an LNT graph posits that any exposure at all is too much and therefore you should seek to not have any exposure, avoiding even the tiniest bit of exposure. You might say it is a zero-tolerance condition (using modern day phrasing). Strictly speaking, if you believe the standardized version of an LNT graph, it means there isn't any level of exposure that is safe.

It is a linear line meaning that it goes straight along a graph (i.e., not a curved line, a straight line), typically at a steep angle like say 45 degrees, proceeding left-to-right, rising up to indicate that the more exposure you receive the worse things will get for you. This linear aspect is usually not the part of the graph that gets the acrimonious arguments underway, instead it is where the line starts on the graph that gets people boiling mad.

In the classic LNT graph, the line starts at the origin point of the graph and the moment that the line starts to rise it is indicating that immediately you are being endangered since any exposure is considered bad. That's the "no-threshold" part of the LNT. There isn't any kind of initial gap or buffer portion that is considered safe. Any exposure is considered unsafe and ill-advised to encounter.

Succinctly stated by Nobel Prize winner Hermann Muller in the 1940s, he was the discoverer of the ability of radiation to cause genetic mutation, and he emphatically stated that radiation is a "no threshold dose" kind of contaminant.

The standard LNT has been a cornerstone of the EPA (Environmental Protection Agency), and a latest twist could be that the classic linear no-threshold might become instead a threshold-based variant. That's kicking up a lot of angst and controversy. By-and-large, the EPA has typically taken the position that any exposure to pollution such as carcinogens is a no-threshold danger, meaning that the substance is dangerous at any level, assuming it is dangerous at some level.

Regulations are usually built on the basis of the no-threshold principle. The EPA has been bolstered by scientists and scientific associations echoing that the standard version of the LNT is a sound and reasonable way to govern on such matters. There is a huge body of research underlying the LNT. It is the foundation of many environmental efforts and safety-related programs in the United States and throughout the globe.

You might at first glance think that this LNT makes a lot of sense. Sure, any exposure to something deadly would seem risky and unwise. Might as well avoid the toxic or endangering item entirely. Case closed.

Not so fast, some say.

There is an argument to be made that sometimes a minor amount of exposure of something is not necessarily that bad, and indeed in some instances it might be considered good.

What might that be, you wonder?

Some would cite drinking and alcohol as an example.

For a long time, health concerns have been raised that drinking alcohol is bad for you, including that it can ruin your liver, it can harm your brain cells, it can become addictive, it can make you fat, it can lead to getting diabetes, it can increase your chances of getting cancer, you can blackout, and so on. The list is rather lengthy. Seems like something that should be avoided, entirely.

Meanwhile, you've likely heard or seen the studies that now say that alcohol can possibly increase your life expectancy, it can overcome undue shyness and enable you to be bolder and more dynamic, and it might reduce your risk of getting heart disease. There are numerous bona fide medical studies that have indicated that drinking red wine, for example, might be able to prevent coronary artery diseases and therefore lessen your chances of getting a heart attack. In essence, there are health-positive benefits presumably to drinking.

I assume that you are quick to retort that those "benefits" of drinking are only when you drink alcohol in moderation and with care. Someone that drinks alcohol too much is certainly likely to experience the "cost" or bad sides of drinking and will be less likely to receive any "gains" regarding the otherwise beneficial aspects of drinking.

One concern you might have about touching on the benefits of drinking is that it might be used by some to justify over-drinking, such as those wild college drinking binges that seem to occur (as a former professor, I had many occasions of students showing up to class that had obviously opted to indulge the night before and they were zombies while in the classroom).

If I asked you to create a graph that indicated how much you would recommend that others can drink, what kind of graph line would you make?

The problem you likely would wrestle with is the notion that if you provide a threshold of drinking, maybe one that allows for a low dosage, say a glass of red wine per day, it could become the proverbial snowball that will roll down the snowy hill and become an avalanche. By allowing any kind of signaling that drinking is Okay, you might be opening up Pandoras box. One glass of wine per day that someone feels comfortable drinking, prompted by your graph, might personally take it upon themselves to gradually enlarge it to two glasses, then it morphs into an oh-so-easy four glasses per day, and onward toward an untoward end.

Perhaps it might be better to just state that no drinking is safe and therefore you can close-off any chance of others trying to wiggle their way into becoming alcoholics by claiming you might have led them down that brim rose path. If you have any kind of allowed threshold, others might try to drive a Mack truck through it and later on say they got hooked into drinking and it ultimately ruined their lives.

You might be tempted therefore to make your graph show a no-threshold indication. This maybe seems harsh as you mull it over, yet if you are trying to "do the right thing" it seems to be the clearest and safest way to portray the matter.

That's pretty much the logic used by the EPA. Historically, the EPA has tended to side with the no-threshold perspective since they have been concerned that allowing any amount of threshold, even a small one, could start the floodgates. They also point out that when trying to make national policy, it is hard to say how exposures can impact any particular person, depending upon their personal characteristics such as age, overall health, and other factors. Thus, the best bet is to make an overarching proclamation that covers presumably everyone, and to do so the no-threshold LNT is the way to do so.

The counter-argument is that this is like the proverbial tossing out the baby with the bath water. You are apparently willing to get rid of the potential "good" for the sake of the potential "bad," and therefore presumably won't have any chance at even experiencing the good. Is the health-positive of having a glass of wine per day so lowly in value that it is fine to discard it and instead make the overly simplified and overly generalized claim that alcohol in any amount is bad for you?

The other counter-argument is that oftentimes the use of the no-threshold approach fails to take into account the costs involved in going along with a no-threshold notion. What kind of cost might there be to enforce the no-threshold rule? It could be extremely expensive to deal with the even small doses portion, yet the small doses might either be not so bad or possibly even good.

You are therefore not only undermining the chances of gaining the good, which we're assuming for the moment happens in the smaller dose's aspects, but you are also raising the costs overall to attain the no-threshold line-in-the-sand.

Some say that if you allowed for a some-threshold model (versus the stringent no-threshold), you could bring back into the picture the good parts of the matter, plus you would potentially cut the costs tremendously that had gone towards achieving this no-threshold burden at the lower threshold level. Those reduced costs might then be placed toward other greater goods and not have to be any further "wasted" by dealing with the small threshold of something that had a goodness in it anyway.

When I've been referring to having a (relatively) small initial threshold, there's a word that commonly is used to refer to such a phenomenon, namely it is called hormesis.

We could take a traditional Linear No-Threshold (LNT) graph, and place onto the graph an indication of a hormesis process, meaning something that allows for having a neutral or possibly positive reaction when at small levels of exposure. The first part of the hormesis's line or curve would showcase that at the low doses, the result is neutral or possibly positive. That area of the line or curve that contains this neural or positive result is considered the hormetic zone.

There is an entire body of research devoted to hormesis and it is a popular word among those that study these kinds of matters.

You can be a hormesis scientist, or if not a scientist of it or devoted to it, you can perhaps be a supporter of the hormesis viewpoint.

It's not something that most of us use or would hear on a daily basis. I'm introducing it herein so that I can proceed henceforth within to refer to the hormetic zone and you'll know I am referring to that part of a graph that indicates the reaction or result of a neutral or positive nature when exposed to something that otherwise at higher levels is considered unsafe or heightened in risk.

Typing this back to the discussion about the EPA, there are some that worry about an emerging rising tide of those supporting hormesis that are now beginning to reshape how the EPA does its environmental efforts and makes its regulations. The traditional no-threshold LNT camp is fiercely battling to keep the hormesis supporters at bay. This comes down to preventing any kind of some-threshold or inclusion of a hermetic zone into the work of the EPA.

I'm not going to weigh into that debate about the EPA and related policy matters (you can track the daily news to keep up with that matter, if you wish).

Here's why I brought it up.

I wanted to bring your attention to the overall notion of the LNT, along with opening your eyes to the debate that can sometimes be waged about whether to allow for any threshold, which some say might is inherently and automatically bad, for the reasons I've mentioned earlier, versus insisting on a no-threshold, which some at times is implied that it "must" be inherently and exclusively good.

Of course, as I've now mentioned, the no-threshold has its own advantages and disadvantages. This is a crucial aspect to realize, since at times the no-threshold is put in place without any realization of it being both a positive and a negative, depending upon what kind of matter we might be discussing.

You should be cautious in falling into a mental trap that the no-threshold versus the some-threshold is always to be won by the no-threshold, and instead ponder the tradeoffs in a given matter of whether the no-threshold or the some-threshold seem to be the better choice.

What does this have to do with AI self-driving cars?

At the Cybernetic AI Self-Driving Car Institute, we are developing AI software for self-driving cars. I am a frequent speaker at industry conferences and one of the most popular questions that I get has to do with the societal and economic rationale for pushing ahead on AI self-driving cars. The crux of the matter involves lives saved versus lives lost. As you'll see in a moment, this is quite related to the Linear No-Threshold (LNT) that I've introduced you to.

Allow me to elaborate.

I'd like to first clarify and introduce the notion that there are varying levels of AI self-driving cars. The topmost level is considered Level 5. A Level 5 self-driving car is one that is being driven by the AI and there is no human driver involved. For the design of Level 5 self-driving cars, the auto makers are even removing the gas pedal, brake pedal, and steering wheel, since those are contraptions used by human drivers. The Level 5 self-driving car is not being driven by a human and nor is there an expectation that a human driver will be present in the self-driving car. It's all on the shoulders of the AI to drive the car.

For self-driving cars less than a Level 5, there must be a human driver present in the car. The human driver is currently considered the responsible party for the acts of the car. The AI and the human driver arc co-sharing the driving task. In spite of this co-sharing, the human is supposed to remain fully immersed into the driving task and be ready at all times to perform the driving task. I've repeatedly warned about the dangers of this co-sharing arrangement and predicted it will produce many untoward results.

Let's focus herein on the true Level 5 self-driving car. Much of the comments apply to the less than Level 5 self-driving cars too, but the fully autonomous AI self-driving car will receive the most attention in this discussion.

Here's the usual steps involved in the AI driving task:

- Sensor data collection and interpretation

- Sensor fusion

- Virtual world model updating

- AI action planning

- Car controls command issuance

Another key aspect of AI self-driving cars is that they will be driving on our roadways in the midst of human driven cars too. There are some pundits of AI self-driving cars that continually refer to a utopian world in which there are only AI self-driving cars on the public roads. Currently there are about 250+ million conventional cars in the United States alone, and those cars are not going to magically disappear or become true Level 5 AI self-driving cars overnight.

Indeed, the use of human driven cars will last for many years, likely many decades, and the advent of AI self-driving cars will occur while there are still human driven cars on the roads. This is a crucial point since this means that the AI of self-driving cars needs to be able to contend with not just other AI self-driving cars, but also contend with human driven cars. It is easy to envision a simplistic and rather unrealistic world in which all AI self-driving cars are politely interacting with each other and being civil about roadway interactions. That's not what is going to be happening for the foreseeable future. AI self-driving cars and human driven cars will need to be able to cope with each other.

Returning to the topic of the Linear No-Threshold (LNT) model, let's consider how the LNT might apply to the matter of AI self-driving cars.

One of the most noted reasons to pursue AI self-driving cars involves the existing dismal statistic that approximately 37,000 deaths occur in conventional car accidents each year in the United States alone, and it is hoped or assumed that the advent of AI self-driving cars will reduce or perhaps completely do away with those annual deaths.

In one sense, pursuit of AI self-driving cars can be likened to a noble cause.

There are of course other reasons to seek the adoption of AI self-driving cars. One often cited reason involves the mobility that could be presumably attained by society as a result of readily available AI self-driving cars. Some suggest that the AI self-driving will democratize mobility and provide a profound impact to those that today are without mobility or have limited access to mobility. It is said that our entire economic system will be reshaped into a mobility-as-a-service economy, and we'll see an incredible boon in ridesharing, far beyond anything that have seen to-date.

Let's though focus on the notion of AI self-driving cars being a life saver by seemingly ensuring that we will no longer have any deaths due to car accidents.

You might ponder for a moment what it is about AI self-driving cars that will apparently avoid deaths via car accidents. The usual answer is that there won't be any more drunk drivers on the roads, since the AI will be doing the driving, and therefore we can eliminate any car accidents resulting from humans that drink and drive.

Likewise, we can seemingly eliminate car accidents due to human error, such as failing to hit the brakes in time to avoid crashing into another car or perhaps into a pedestrian.

These human errors might arise because a human driver is distracted while driving, looking at their cell phone or trying to watch a video, and thus they are not attentive to the driving situation. It could also be that humans get into deadly car accidents by getting overly emotional and do not dispassionately make decisions when they are driving. And so on.

For the moment, I'll hesitantly say that we can agree that those kinds of deaths due to car accidents can be eliminated by the use of AI self-driving cars, though I make this concession with reservations in doing so.

My reservations are multi-fold.

For example, as mentioned earlier, we are going to have a mixture of human driven cars and AI self-driving cars for quite a long time to come, and thus it will not be as though there are only AI self-driving cars on the public roadways. The assumption about the elimination of car accidents is partially predicated on the removal of human drivers and human driving, and it doesn't seem like that will happen anytime soon.

Even if we somehow remove all human driving and human drivers from the equation of driving, this does not mean that we would necessarily end-up at zero fatalities in terms of AI self-driving cars. As I've repeatedly emphasized in my writings and presentations, goals of having zero fatalities sound good, but the reality is that there is a zero chance of it. When an AI self-driving car is going down a street at 45 miles per hour, let's assume completely legally doing so, and a pedestrian steps suddenly and unexpectedly into the street, with only a split second before impact, the physics bely any action that the AI self-driving car can take to avoid hitting and likely killing that pedestrian.

You might right away and object and point out that the frequency of those kinds of car accidents involving deaths will certainly be a lot less than it likely does today with conventional cars and human drivers. I would tend to agree. Let's be clear, I am not saying that the number of car related deaths won't likely decrease, and hopefully by a wide margin. Instead, I am saying that the chances of having zero car-related deaths is the questionable proposition.

If you accept that premise, it should then suddenly seem familiar, since it takes us back to my earlier discussion about Linear No-Threshold (LNT) graphs and models.

I'd like to walk you through the type of debate that I usually encounter when discussing this aspect of car-related deaths and AI self-driving cars.

Much of the time, those involved in the debate are not considering the full range of logical perspectives on the matter. Obviously, any discussion about life or death is bound to be fraught with emotionally laden qualms. It is hard to consider in the abstract the idea of deaths that might be due to car accidents. When I get into these discussions, I usually suggest that we think of this as though we are actuary's, tasked with considering how to establish rates for life insurance. It might seem ghoulish, but the role of an actuary is to dispassionately think about deaths, such as their frequency and how they arise.

Take a look at my Figure 1 that shows the range of logical perspectives on this matter of lives and deaths related to AI self-driving cars.

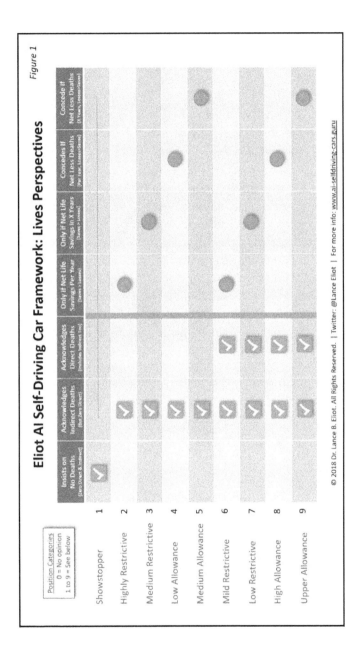

Eliot AI Self-Driving Car Framework: Lives Perspectives

Figure 1

We'll start this discussion by considering those that insist on absolutely no deaths to be permitted by any AI self-driving car. Ever.

Under no circumstances do they see a rationalization for an AI self-driving car being involved in the death of a human. These are diehards that typically say that until AI self-driving cars have proven themselves to never lead to a human death, only then will they support the possibility of AI self-driving cars being on our roadways.

That's quite a harsh position to take.

You could say that it is a no-threshold position. This is comparable to suggesting that the toxicity (in a sense) of an AI self-driving car must be zero before it can be allowed on our roads. The person taking this stance is standing on the absolutely and utterly "no risks" allowed side of things. For them, a Linear No-Threshold (LNT) graph would be a fitting depiction of their viewpoint about AI self-driving cars.

I'd like to qualify the aspect of the LNT in their case is somewhat different than say radiation or a toxic chemical. They are willing to allow AI self-driving cars once they have presumably been "perfected" and are guaranteed (somehow?) to not cause or produce any car-related deaths.

This position would be that you can keep trying to perfect AI self-driving cars in other ways, just not on the public roadways.

Test those budding AI self-driving cars on special closed-tracks that are made for the purposes of advancing AI self-driving cars. Use extensive and large-scale computer-based simulations to try and iron out the kinks. Do whatever can be done, except for being on public roadways, and when that's been done, and in-theory the AI self-driving car is finally ready for death-free driving on the public streets, it can be released into the wild.

The auto makers and tech firms claim that without using AI self-driving cars on the public roadways, there will either not be viable AI self-driving cars until a far distant future, or it might not ever come to pass at all. Without the rigors of being on public roadway, it is assumed that there is no viable way to fully ready AI self-driving cars for public roadways. It is a kind of Catch-22. If you won't allow AI self-driving cars on public roadways, you are either won't ever have them there or it will be many moons from now.

For those that are in the camp of no-deaths, they reply that go ahead and take whatever time you need. If it takes 20 years, 50 years, a thousand years, and you still aren't ready for the public roadways, so be it. That's the price to pay for ensuring the no-deaths perspective.

But this seems reminiscent once again of the LNT argument.

Suppose that while you wait for AI self-driving cars to be perfected, meanwhile those 37,000 deaths per year with conventional cars is continuing unabated. If you wait say 50 years for AI self-driving cars to be perfected, you are also presumably offering that you are willing to have perhaps nearly 200,000 people die during that period of time. This usually causes the no-deaths camp to become irate, since they are certainly not saying that they are callously discounting those deaths.

This hopefully moves the discussion into one that attempts to see both sides of the equation. There are presumably deaths or lives to be saved, as a result of the adoption of AI self-driving cars, though it is conceivable that those AI self-driving cars will still nonetheless be attributable to some amount of car-related deaths.

Are you willing or not to seek the "good" savings of lives (or reductions in deaths), in exchange for the lives (or deaths) that will be lost while AI self-driving cars are on our roadways and being perfected (if there is such a thing)?

If you could get to AI self-driving cars sooner, such as in 10 years, during which in-theory without any AI self-driving cars on the roadways you would have lost say 370,000 lives, would you do so, if you also were willing to allow for some number of car-related deaths that were attributable to the still being perfected AI self-driving cars. That's the rub.

The "showstopper" perspective, shown as the first row of my chart, would continue to embrace the no-deaths permitted via AI self-driving cars notion and either not see the apparent logic of the aforementioned, or be dubious that there is any kind of net savings of lives to be had. They might argue that it could horribly turnout that the number of lives lost, as a result of the initial tryout and perfecting period of AI self-driving cars, might overwhelm the number of lives that were presumably going to be saved.

I'd like to broaden the idea too of AI self-driving cars and car-related deaths that might occur, just to get everything clearly onto the table. I'm going to consider direct deaths and also indirect deaths.

There are direct deaths, such as an AI self-driving car that rear-ends another car, and either a human in the rammed car dies or a human passenger in the AI self-driving car dies (or, of course, it could be multiple human deaths), and for which we could investigate the matter and perhaps agree that it was the fault of the AI self-driving car. Maybe the AI self-driving car had a bug in it, or maybe it was confused due to a sensor that failed, or a myriad of things might have gone wrong.

There are indirect deaths that can also occur. Suppose an AI self-driving car swerves into an adjacent lane on the freeway. There's a car in that lane, and the driver gets caught off-guard and slams on their brakes to avoid hitting the lane-changing AI self-driving car. Meanwhile, the car behind the brake-slamming car is approaching at a fast rate of speed and collides with the braking car. This car, last in the sequence, rolls over and the human occupants are killed.

I refer to this as an indirect death.

The AI self-driving car was not directly involved in the death, though it was a significant contributing factor. We'd need to sort out why the AI self-driving car made the sudden lane change, and why and how the other cars were being driven to figure out the blame aspects. In any case, I'm going to count this kind of scenario as one in which an AI self-driving gets involved in a death related incident, even though it might not have been the AI self-driving that directly generated the human death.

There's the first row, the showstopper, consisting of the no-deaths perspective. This viewpoint is that under no circumstances at all will they be satisfied with having AI self-driving cars on the public roadway, until or if they are assured that doing so will cause absolutely no deaths. This encompasses both the no indirect deaths and the posture of no direct deaths. This viewpoint also is blind to the net lives that might be saved, during an interim period of AI self-driving cars being on the roadway and won't consider the net lives saved and nor the net less deaths possibilities.

That's about as pure a version of a no-threshold belief as you can find.

Some criticize that camp and use the old proverb that perfection is the enemy of good. By not allowing AI self-driving cars to be on our public roadways until they are somehow guaranteed not to produce any deaths, indirect or direct, you are apparently seeking perfection and will meanwhile be denying a potential good along the way. Plus, maybe the good won't ever materialize because of that same stance.

For the remainder of the chart, I provide eight variations of those that would be considered the some-threshold camp. This takes us into the hormetic zone.

Yes, I bring up once again the hormetic zone. In this case, it would be the zone during which AI self-driving cars might be allowed onto the roadways and doing so might provide a "good" to society, and yet we would acknowledge that there will also be a "bad" in that those AI self-driving cars are going to produce car-related deaths.

There are four distinct stances or positions about indirect deaths (see the chart rows numbered as 2, 3, 4, 5), and are all instances that involve a willingness to "accept" the possibility of incurring indirect deaths due to AI self-driving cars being on the roadways during this presumed interim period.

For the columns, there is the situation of a belief that there will be a net savings of lives (the number of lives "saved" from the predicted number of usual deaths is greater than the number of indirect deaths generated via the AI self-driving cars), or there will be a net less-deaths (the number of indirect deaths will be greater than the number of lives "saved" in comparison to the predicted number of usual deaths).

One tricky and argumentative aspect about the counting of net lives or net deaths is the time period that you would use to do so.

There are some that would say they would only tolerate this matter if the aggregate count in any given year produces the net savings. Thus, if AI self-driving cars are allowed onto our roadways, it means that in each year that this takes place, the net lives saved must bear out in that year. Every year.

This though might be problematic. If we picked a longer period of time, say some X number of years (use 5 years as a plug-in example), maybe the net savings would come out as you hoped, though during those five years there might have been any of those particular years that the net savings was actually be a net loss.

Would you be so restrictive that it had to be just per-year, or would you be willing to take a longer time period of some kind and be satisfied if the numbers came out over that overall time period – you decide.

Per my chart, we have these four positions about indirect deaths:

- Highly Restrictive = indirect deaths with net life savings each year mandatory (savings > losses)

- Medium Restrictive = indirect deaths with net life savings over X years (where X > 1, savings > losses)

- Low Allowance = indirect deaths with net less deaths each year mandatory (losses > savings)

- Medium Allowance = indirect deaths with net less deaths over X years (where X > 1, losses > savings)

I realize you might be concerned and confounded about the notion of having net less deaths. Why would anyone agree to something that involves the number of losses due to AI self-driving cars being greater than the number of lives "saved" by the use of AI self-driving cars? The answer is that during this hormetic zone, we are assuming that this is something that might indeed occur, and we are presumably willing to allow it in exchange for the future lives savings that will arise once we get out of the hormetic zone.

Without seeming to be callous, take the near-term pain to achieve the longer-term gain, some might argue.

To get a "fairer" picture of the matter, you should presumably count the ongoing number of lives saved, forever after, once you get out of the hormetic zone, and plug that back into your numbers.

Let's say it takes 10 years to get out of the hormetic zone, and then thereafter we have AI self-driving cars for the next say 100 years, and during that time the number of predicted deaths by conventional cars would be entirely (or nearly so) avoided. If so, using a macroscopic view of the matter, you should take the 100 years' worth of potential deaths that were avoided, so that's 100 x 37,000, which comes to 3,700,000 deaths avoided, and add those back into the hormetic zone years.

It certainly makes the hormetic zone period likely more palatable. This requires a willingness to make a lot of assumptions about the future and might be difficult for most people to find credible.

The remain four positions are about direct deaths. It would seem that anyone likely willing to consider direct deaths would also be willing to consider indirect deaths, and thus it makes sense to lump together the indirect and direct deaths for these remaining categories.

Here they are:

- Mild Restrictive = direct + indirect deaths with net life savings each year mandatory (savings > losses)

- Low Restrictive = direct + indirect deaths with net life savings over X years (where X > 1, savings > losses)

- High Allowance = direct + indirect deaths with net less deaths each year mandatory (losses > savings)

- Upper Allowance = direct + indirect deaths with net less deaths over X years (where X > 1, losses > savings)

You can use this overall chart to engage someone into a hopefully intelligent debate about the advent of AI self-driving cars, doing so without a lot of hand waving and yelling that seems ill-served, amorphous, lacks structure, and often seems to generate more heat than substance.

I usually begin by ferreting out whether the person is taking the showstopper stance, in which case there is not much to discuss, assuming that they have actually thought about all of the other positions. It could be that they have not considered those other positions, and upon doing so, they will adjust their mindset and begin find another posture that fits to their sensibility on the matter.

If someone is more open to the matter and willing to discuss the hormetic zone notion of the adoption of AI self-driving cars, you are likely to then find you and the other person anguishing over trying to identify the magic number X.

The person is potentially willing to be in any of the camps numbered 2 through 9, but they are unsure because of the time period that might be involved. Were X to be a somewhat larger number, such as say a dozen years, they might find it very hard to go along with the net less deaths and be only willing to go along with the net savings, and also they might say they want this to be per year, rather than aggregated over the entire time period. For an X that is lesser in size, perhaps 5 or less, they are at times more open to the other positions.

The handy thing about this chart overall and the approach is that it gets the debate onto firmer ground. No wild finger pointing needed. Instead, calmly try to see this as an actuarial kind of exercise. In doing so, consider what each of the chart positions suggests.

I usually hold back a few other notable aspects that I figure can regrettably turn the discussion nearly immediately upside down.

For example, suppose that we never reach this nirvana of perfected AI self-driving cars, in spite of perhaps allowed them to be used on our public roadways, and in the end they are still going to be involved in car-related deaths. That's a lot to take in.

Also, as I earlier mentioned, it is not especially realistic to suggest that AI self-driving cars won't be involved in any car-related deaths, ever, even once so-called perfection is reached, per the example I gave of the pedestrian that unexpectedly steps in front of an AI self-driving car coming down the street.

In that instance, I'm saying that the AI self-driving was working "perfectly" and noticed the pedestrian, and ascertain the pedestrian was standing still, on the curb, and the self-driving car was going to drive past the pedestrian, just like any of us human drivers would, and the pedestrian without any sufficient warning jumps into the street.

The physics involved preclude the AI self-driving car of doing anything other than hitting the pedestrian.

Yes, maybe the brakes are applied or the AI self-driving car attempts to swerve away, but if the pedestrian does this with no warning and only a few feet in front of the AI self-driving car, there's no braking or swerving that would be done in sufficient time to avoid the matter.

How many of those kinds of "perfected" AI self-driving car related car-deaths will we have? It's hard to say. I've previously warned that we are going to have pranks by humans toward AI self-driving cars, which indeed has already been occurring. It could be that some humans will try to trick an AI self-driving car and get killed while doing so. There might be other instances of humans not paying attention and getting run over, not because of a prank and simply because it happens in the real-world that we live in.

Conclusion

Whether you know it or not, we are currently in the hormetic zone. AI self-driving cars are already on our public roadways.

So far, most of the tryouts include a human back-up driver, but as I've repeatedly stated, a human back-up driver does not translate into a guarantee that an AI self-driving car is not going to be involved in a car-related death. The Uber self-driving car incident in Arizona is an example of that unfortunate point.

Per my predictions about the upcoming status of AI self-driving cars, we are headed toward an inflexion point. There are going to be more deaths involving AI self-driving cars, including direct and indirect deaths.

How many such deaths will be tolerated before the angst causes the public and regulators to decide to bring down the hammer on AI self-driving cars tryouts on our roadways?

If the threshold is going to be a small number such as one death or two deaths, it pretty much means that AI self-driving cars will no longer be considered viable on our public roadways.

This then means that it will be up to using closed-tracks and simulations to try and "perfect" AI self-driving cars.

Yet, as per my earlier points, the pell-mell rush to get AI self-driving cars possibly off the roadways could dampen the pace of advancing AI self-driving cars, which as mentioned could imply that we'll be incurring conventional car deaths that much longer.

Can the public and regulators view this advent of AI self-driving cars as an LNT type of problem?

Is there room to shift from a no-threshold to some-threshold?

Can the use of hormesis approaches give guidance of looking at a larger picture?

As an aside, one unfortunate element of referring to LNT is that it in a sense is not well regarded by those that are dealing with truly toxic substances, and for which they tend to make the case that indeed no-threshold is the way to go. I don't want to overplay the LNT analogy since I don't want others to somehow ascribe to AI self-driving cars that they are a type of radiation or carcinogen that needs to be abated. Please do keep that in mind.

Can the scourge of any deaths at the "hands" of an AI self-driving car be tolerated as long as there is progress toward reducing conventional cars deaths?

It's a lot for anyone to consider.

It certainly isn't going to lend itself to a debate in 140-characters at a time basis. It's more complex than that.

Might as well start thinking about the threshold problem right now, since we'll soon enough find ourselves completely immersed in the soup of it. Things are undoubtedly coming to come to a boil.

CHAPTER 3
PREDICTION EQUATION
AND
AI SELF-DRIVING CARS

CHAPTER 3

PREDICTION EQUATION
AND
AI SELF-DRIVING CARS

We all enjoy a good equation.

How many times have you quoted or seen Einstein's famous equation about matter and energy? Many times, I would wager.

I'm assuming most of you likely memorized ad nauseum the Pythagorean Theorem of a-squared plus b-squared equals c-squared. Like it or not, the Pythagorean equation is a crucial building block for mathematics and infuses geometry and calculus (you likely haven't used it in a while, and my bringing it up might trigger either pleasant memories of your math classes or cause you undue angst, oops).

One of the most famous probabilistic formulas is the celebrated Drake equation, which was devised by Frank Drake in the 1960s to help stir discussion and debate about the odds that there is life elsewhere in our galaxy and that we might be able to communicate with it. Some of you might be aware of the SETI (Search for Extraterrestrial Intelligence) program that actively is scanning for any sign from another planet that someone or something out there might exist. We here on earth are using various electronic and computer-based means to detect signals from outer space.

A particularly controversial element of such efforts is whether or not we should be undertaking a passive search or a more active search for intelligent life that might elsewhere exist. A passive search involves the act of simply trying to catch ahold of any signals and then be on-earth internally alerted that perhaps something is out there. An active search consists of sending out a signal to let the beyond-our-planet listeners know that we are here, and we do so in hopes of sparking a response. Of course, generating a response might be good or bad for us and the renowned Stephen Hawking had forewarned that we might stir-up a hornet's nest that will ultimately cause our own destruction and demise.

There are some that say there's little or no chance of any intelligence existing out there in our galaxy. Indeed, they would say that the chances are so low of such an existence that it is a waste of time and attention to be searching for it. Use our resources for other more worldly and sensible pursuits, they would assert. Plus, if by some bizarre chance there is something out there, the active search method is crazily dangerous and thus at least let's stop any attempts to prod or poke the unseen and unheard from beast.

I realize to some this seems like speaking from both sides of their mouths in that they on the one hand are saying that there's essentially no chance of anything out there, yet they also are willing to fret about poking it into awareness of us, but they would counter-argue that it is merely prudent to not do something that is unwise, even if the odds of the unwise act being fruitful are near to nil.

What is the chance of there being intelligent life somewhere in our galaxy other than here on earth, you might be pondering?

As an aside, there are usually wisecracks about the assumption that we here are intelligent life, and you can try to make that joke if you like, it's mildly funny, I suppose, and you can also seek to debate whether we are "intelligent" at all and maybe there are other life forms out there that are a zillion times more intelligent than us, etc.

I'm not going to entertain those debates herein and merely lay claim that we are intelligent and that yes there might be other intelligent life forms, including ones that might be well-beyond us in terms of some kind of super-intelligence. Those super intelligent beings, if they exist, do not ergo mean that we aren't intelligent at all, and their existence would instead just push our own self-inflated belief about our being intelligent into realizing we are of a lesser intelligence (and yet still retain the classification of being intelligent), I suggest.

Back to the question about the odds of intelligent life beyond us.

Let's first agree that we're primarily interested in intelligent life, meaning that if there is some kind of primitive life oozing someplace and for which it or they cannot communicate in any modern means, we'll set those aside as being unworthy for the moment of trying to find. Sure, we'd keenly like to know that there is something percolating, though this is a lot less interesting overall than finding something already up-and-running that exhibits intelligence as we think today of the notion of being intelligent.

Presumably, an intelligent life form would be emitting various kinds of electromagnetic radiation, doing so as we indeed do here on earth. That intelligence might not be emitting the radiation for purposes of letting others know that they exist, and might simply be making the emissions as a natural act of how they live, similar to how we watch TV and use our cellphones (I assume most of us do so for our own benefit, and not due to hopes of signaling to other life forms that we exist).

Astronomer Frank Drake had been using a large-scale radio astronomical device in West Virginia in the late 1950s to scan for radio waves bouncing off our planet. His project was somewhat initiated due to ongoing debates at the time about whether or not there could be life anywhere else other than earth. Some said the idea of other life elsewhere was ludicrous. Some suggested that even if there was life elsewhere, it might be early in its development and therefore not yet sophisticated enough to communicate, either by intent or by happenstance.

There were numbers floating around by scientists and astronomers especially that there might be 100 million worlds in the universe that could sustain life as we know of it. How did the 100 million number come to be derived? It was based on the belief that there might be 10 million million million suns, and perhaps one in a million of those suns that had various planets revolving around the sun, and of those perhaps one in a million million that were planets composed of the needed aspects to foster life. If you multiply that out, you arrive at the handy number of 100 million planets that in-theory could have life on it.

Frank Drake opted to put together a small conference of those keenly interested in the serious pursuit of intelligent life and hoped to get vigorous discussion going. In preparing for the conference, he decided to jot down a means to predict the odds of there being intelligent life in our galaxy. Using the same kind of logic that had been used to create the 100 million planets number of the universe, he thought it might be handy to write down the factors and craft an equation that all could see and chat about. The equation was intended for shaping debates and not an attempt to arrive at some kind of magical equation such as Einstein's famous $E = MC^2$.

The equation that Frank presented has since then become famously known as the Drake equation, giving due credit to his having derived it. Over the years, there have been many that point out the equation as failing to include a number of other factors that should presumably be included. That's fine and it was not Frank's assertion that his equation was the end-all be-all. Today there are a slew of variants and many have added more factors, while some have altered his stated factors. You might say it is a living equation in that it continues to foster debate and continues to generate other formulas that could be better (or worse) than his original stipulation.

Frank Drake's equation consists of trying to arrive at a number N, which would purport to be the number of civilizations within our galaxy that might exhibit intelligence and for which it might be possible to communicate with them.

You can argue somewhat that suppose there are intelligent life forms that are hiding and purposely not wanting to communicate with us, and you can also quibble with the idea that suppose there are multiple intelligent life forms on any given planet and does that count as one or maybe several such counts, and so on. Generally, the number N is going to be large enough that we can set aside those rounding error kind of exceptions and just contemplate the magnitude of the number N itself.

Here's the Drake equation: N = R-star x Factor p x Factor ne x Factor 1 x Factor i x Factor c x Factor L

Essentially, you multiply together seven key factors and it will get you to the number N. Each of the factors is logically sensible in terms of what you would expect to consider when making this kind of an estimate. The factors tend to build upon each other, doing so in the manner of considering a type of pie, wherein you might slice up a pie, doing so incrementally until you get to the final slice.

This is reminiscent of the earlier indicated 100 million number.

You might recall it was derived by first considering the whole pie, namely how many total planets might there be in the entire universe (as based on the number of suns and how many planets they might have). Then, the pie was sliced-up by estimating how many of those planets might sustain life.

Drake's equation does the same thing and takes the estimate deeper by slicing further to how many of those life forms might arise to intelligent beings, and how many of those might arise to intelligent beings that emit some kind of signal that we could detect such as maybe watching TV or using their smartphones (or whatever).

Let's consider each of the factors in the Drake equation.

- The R-star is an estimate of the average rate of star formulations within our galaxy.

- The Factor p is the fraction of those R number of stars that would likely have planets.

- The Factor ne is the estimated average number of those planets that could support life.

- The Factor 1 is the estimated fraction of those planets that could develop life as based on the planets supporting the emergence of life forms.

- The Factor i is an estimate of how many of those planets that are able to develop life then produce intelligent life (which we'll refer to as civilizations).

- The Factor c is the estimated fraction of those that have intelligent life for which they make use of some kind of technology that produces emissions of which we could detect.

- The Factor L is the estimated length of time in years that the intelligent life that is emitting such emissions does so.

I hope you can see that the Drake equation is actually quite simple and readily digested. I am not denigrating the formula by saying so. In fact, I applaud the equation for its ease of comprehension.

Had the formula been arcane, I doubt that it would have gained such widespread interest and popularity.

I'll also mention that it is interesting that it has seven factors, rather than say a dozen or perhaps two dozen or more. When you consider the other kinds of factors you might want to include, this equation could easily grow to be a long list of factors. The beauty of having just seven factors is that the equation is kept to a core set that is again readily understood.

Plus, it conforms to the equally famous indication in cognitive psychology that we humans prefer things that are about seven items, plus or minus two items, which was identified by George Miller in his well-known paper in 1956 that appeared in the journal Psychology Review.

Another fascinating aspect is that the factors are all multiplied together. Again, this suggests simplicity. If the factors involved doing complex transformations and using say square roots or a multitude of additions and divisions, it would be difficult to readily calculate and would be confusing to the naked eye. Instead, you've got a series of straightforward factors and they are multiplied together to arrive at the sought number N.

The factors appear to be simple and the equation appears to be simple, which makes it ideal for being used and discussed. Meanwhile, let's all agree that coming up with the numbers that go into those factors is a bit more challenging. The numbers that you plug into the factors are going to be estimates. Those estimates are going to potentially spur tremendous debate.

In fact, most of the debates about Drake's equation is not the equation per se, but instead the estimates that one might plug into the factors of the equation. That there is disagreement about the estimates is not especially unnerving, nor does it somehow undermine the equation itself. You need a lot of science to come up with the estimates. There can be bona fide disagreement about how you come up with the estimates and whether they are any good or not.

What was the N that Drake and his colleagues came up with in 1961, based on his formula? Well, the group decided a range would be the more prudent way to express N, and they generally arrived at a vale of between 1,000 and 100,000,000.

You might be puzzled at the range, since it obviously seems like a rather large range. Here on earth, if I told you that the number of cows on a farm ranged from one thousand to perhaps one-hundred million, you'd think I had gone nuts. One-thousand is a pretty small number, while one-hundred million cows is a humungous number (imagine how much milk you could produce!).

In defense of the estimated range, you could say that they came up with a number greater than zero and that it is also less than some truly large number such as estimates into the billions. Of course, some would claim that the "correct" number is so close to zero that it might was well be considered zero (these are the claimants that say there is no other intelligent life out there that is in a posture to somehow communicate with us).

People have played quite a bit with the Drake equation and its estimates. I mentioned earlier that you could propose to include additional factors, or modify existing factors, or drop-out some of the factors. Likewise, you can do all sorts of variants on how to arrive at the estimated values that plug into the factors. Numerous studies that use Monte Carlo models and simulate varying estimates have suggested that the N can vary rather wildly.

I'd say that the Drake equation was immensely successful in being able to get your arms around the question of whether or not there is intelligent life out there that we might be able to communicate with. Regardless of how "good" the equation is, and regardless of how hard or wildly differing the estimates of the factors are, there is nonetheless a healthy ongoing dialogue on the topic.

If we didn't have a Drake equation it would make things immensely difficult to have a discussion on the topic at-hand about intelligent life elsewhere. Everyone would be waving their arms and not be able to be specific to the topic. Overall, the Drake equation highlights the value of having a kind of anchor, around which discussion can grow and mature.

Not having an anchor tends to ferment discourse that is obtuse and wandering when debating complex matters and particularly when there is heated and divergent views.

Having an anchor is like planting a tree, and you can then watch as additional discourse grows around it.

What does this have to do with AI self-driving cars?

At the Cybernetic AI Self-Driving Car Institute, we are developing AI software for self-driving cars. One of the most outspoken national and worldwide debates involves when AI self-driving cars will be "here" in terms of being available for use. This question continually arises at conferences and by those within this field, along with it being asked by the general public, and by regulators, and by many other stakeholders.

I propose that we derive a kind of Drake equation to aid in the debate. Allow me to elaborate.

I'd like to first clarify and introduce the notion that there are varying levels of AI self-driving cars. The topmost level is considered Level 5. A Level 5 self-driving car is one that is being driven by the AI and there is no human driver involved. For the design of Level 5 self-driving cars, the auto makers are even removing the gas pedal, brake pedal, and steering wheel, since those are contraptions used by human drivers. The Level 5 self-driving car is not being driven by a human and nor is there an expectation that a human driver will be present in the self-driving car. It's all on the shoulders of the AI to drive the car.

For self-driving cars less than a Level 5, there must be a human driver present in the car. The human driver is currently considered the responsible party for the acts of the car. The AI and the human driver are co-sharing the driving task. In spite of this co-sharing, the human is supposed to remain fully immersed into the driving task and be ready at all times to perform the driving task. I've repeatedly warned about the dangers of this co-sharing arrangement and predicted it will produce many untoward results.

Let's focus herein on the true Level 5 self-driving car. Much of the comments apply to the less than Level 5 self-driving cars too, but the fully autonomous AI self-driving car will receive the most attention in this discussion.

Here's the usual steps involved in the AI driving task:

- Sensor data collection and interpretation

- Sensor fusion

- Virtual world model updating

- AI action planning

- Car controls command issuance

Another key aspect of AI self-driving cars is that they will be driving on our roadways in the midst of human driven cars too. There are some pundits of AI self-driving cars that continually refer to a utopian world in which there are only AI self-driving cars on the public roads. Currently there are about 250+ million conventional cars in the United States alone, and those cars are not going to magically disappear or become true Level 5 AI self-driving cars overnight.

Indeed, the use of human driven cars will last for many years, likely many decades, and the advent of AI self-driving cars will occur while there are still human driven cars on the roads. This is a crucial point since this means that the AI of self-driving cars needs to be able to contend with not just other AI self-driving cars, but also contend with human driven cars.

It is easy to envision a simplistic and rather unrealistic world in which all AI self-driving cars are politely interacting with each other and being civil about roadway interactions. That's not what is going to be happening for the foreseeable future. AI self-driving cars and human driven cars will need to be able to cope with each other.

Returning to the topic of predicting the advent of AI self-driving cars, let's consider the characteristics of an equation that could aid in such an important endeavor.

First, consider the matter of who makes predictions about the advent of AI self-driving cars.

There are various technologists that offer their opinions about AI self-driving cars and proffer when we'll see those vehicles on our streets and byways. One upside about technologists is that they hopefully are versed in the technology and are able to judge the efficacy of how AI and autonomous capabilities are progressing. Not all such tech-related prognosticators are particularly versed in the specifics of AI self-driving cars and so they are merely from afar trying to guess at what is happening, which I at times find to be an overreach on their part and can see that they are actually ill-informed on the matter (worse still, others that are not in high-tech arena assume that these false or misinformed prophets do know what they are talking about!).

They should stick to their knitting.

Let's also though consider that those technologists truly versed in AI self-driving cars and making predictions might do so without any tangible rhyme or reason. Sometimes they make a "gut" or instinct proclamation. Sometimes they are so enamored by the allure of AI self-driving cars that they are overly optimistic and make predictions based on emotional excitement more so than serious thought.

Throughout the history of technology, we've certainly seen quite a number of rather overly optimistic predictions that did not come to fruition in the time frame offered.

It's an easy trap to fall into. There's the classic 80/20 rule that the first 80% of something is easy or easier to get accomplished and the last 20% is arduous. Heady technologists will often experience the first 80% and extrapolate that the remaining 20% will proceed at the same pace. This often is not the case. It's the last-mile problem of getting the hardest parts done at the end of the journey.

We also need to clarify that technology in the case of AI self-driving cars can cut both ways, presenting capabilities to achieve autonomy, but also inhibiting autonomy due to the lack of as-yet known approaches, techniques, and computing tools. As such, I find it useful to consider technological advances and how they are formulating, while also considering technological obstacles that are known are even unknown and will be discovered further down the road.

Many technologists that make predictions often do not include other seemingly non-tech related factors that can mightily impact the pace of technology. This is a delinquency of omission, one might say.

What kind of factors will affect the advent of AI self-driving cars?

There are economic factors that will either encourage spending on the development of AI self-driving cars or might dampen and undermine such spending if pulled away and used for other purposes. I've stated many times in my writings and presentations that one of the reasons that we're seeing the rapid progress of AI self-driving cars is due to the money. Yes, follow the money, as they say. Prior to the monies now flowing into the development of AI self-driving cars, there wasn't much being spent on it, other than dribbles and drabs, often in the form of research grants for university labs.

Another key factor is society and societal acceptance or resistance to the advent of AI self-driving cars.

There could be a tough choice to be made about the progress for AI self-driving cars in terms of unleashing them onto our public roadways, and yet at the same time having them get involved into deadly car accidents. Will society accept the idea that to make progress there is a need to put AI self-driving cars onto our streets and yet those AI systems and self-driving cars might produce injuries or fatalities while still being tested and polished? Maybe yes, maybe not.

It is also crucial to consider the regulatory environment and how it can impact the advent of AI self-driving cars. Currently, regulations about using AI self-driving cars on our public roadways is relatively loose and encourages this budding innovation. If regulators are suddenly pressured to do something about AI self-driving cars, such as when deaths or injuries arise while the self-driving cars on the roads, it could quickly swing toward a tightened regulatory setting.

I trust that you are now convinced that any equation trying to predict the advent of AI self-driving cars should not rely solely on a technologist perspective alone. We would want to include the economic perspective, a societal perspective, and a regulatory perspective too. This provides a mixture of perspectives and will hopefully avoid getting caught unawares or blindsided when using solely a single factor.

Each of these factors is not necessarily independent of the other. In fact, the odds are they will tend to swing in the same direction together, though at times on a delayed basis.

For example, suppose the AI of an AI self-driving car is insufficient and makes a computing decision that produces a dramatic and headline catching fatality while driving on a freeway. This could turn public opinion sour. If the public gets extremely sour, regulators are likely to be pushed into or opt to volunteer to set things straight, doing so by making regulations more restrictive on AI self-driving cars. If the regulators get more restrictive, and if public opinion is negative, the auto makers and tech firms might pull back from pouring monies and resources into developing AI self-driving cars.

In exploring the set of factors, you might argue that each factor can end-up being a proponent for and propelling forward AI self-driving cars, or each factor can be an opponent that tends to cause resistance or a dampening to the advent of AI self-driving cars. This is a push-pull kind of tension. It would be vital to encompass this tension in the factors that are used in an equation for making such predictions.

Besides the core factors, there are other matters to be considered.

When someone says that AI self-driving cars are nearly here, I often ask what they mean by "AI self-driving cars" in terms of the levels of capabilities. They might be referring to say Level 3, which in my book is not what I consider a true AI self-driving car. They might even be referring to a Level 4, which I concede is closer to a true AI self-driving car, but I still argue it is not the AI self-driving car level that most people informally are thinking about. To me, Level 5 is the true AI self-driving car.

So, for the purposes of the equation, let's assume that we are trying to predict the advent of true AI self-driving cars at the Level 5 of the accepted standard.

I'd like to also mention that we need to agree on what it means to have an advent of something. If you could make one AI self-driving car at a Level 5, have you achieved reaching an "advent" of that item? No, I don't think so. Though you might have done a great job and arrived at Level 5 instance, until we have some semblance of those AI self-driving cars driving around, it seems questionable to say that there is an advent of them.

How many then is an advent? If there are dozens of true AI self-driving cars traveling on our streets, would that be an advent, or do we need more like hundreds, or maybe thousands. What is the number at which we would have a prevalence of true AI self-driving cars?

There are various ways to measure the prevalence. I'm going to keep things simplified and suggest that we use as a measure the percentage of cars in-use at the time.

We will gradually see a switchover to AI self-driving cars, as mentioned earlier, and this will see the retirement of conventional cars and the rising population of AI self-driving cars.

Of the total population of all cars, we might agree that once a certain percentage becomes true AI self-driving cars, we have reached a prevalence. Assuming you are willing to go along with that premise, we can then debate whether it is 1%, 10%, 20%, 30%, 40%, 50%, 60%, 70%, 80%, 90%, or possibly even 100% before you would refer to it as a prevalence (I used rounded numbers by the tens, but it of course could be any number of 1% to 100%).

I'm going to use 20% for now. Why? In various areas of study, 20% is often used to indicate a prevalence. This comes from environmental and often biological areas of research. It seems like a large enough percentage that it is isn't trivial, and yet not so large that it seems somewhat impossible to reach. For those of you that were thinking more along the lines of a majority, such as reaching 51% or something like it, I certainly understand your viewpoint. Likewise, for those of you that were thinking of 90% or maybe 99%, I grasp that too. In any case, for now, I'm going to use 20%.

In the case of the existing number of conventional cars in the United States, which as mentioned is around 250 million, an advent of AI self-driving cars would at 20% be a rather daunting 50 million such cars. That's a daunting number because think about how long it would likely take to reach that number. In other words, even if AI self-driving cars were immediately ready tomorrow, it would take a while to produce that many self-driving cars, along with a while for those AI self-driving cars to be purchased and put into use.

I've previously predicted that once we do achieve true AI self-driving cars, there is likely going to be a rather rapid adoption rate. I say this because those true AI self-driving cars are going to be money makers.

When there is money to be made, the demand will go through the roof. This is not just fleets of cars, but as I've argued there will be an entire cottage industry of individual consumers that will buy AI self-driving cars to leverage those vehicles as both personal use and for making money.

I've now laid the groundwork for making an equation that can be used to predict the advent of AI self-driving cars.

The last piece to the puzzle is coming up with a base of when the advent might be reached. By using a base, you can then multiply it by the various factors and see whether the resulting N is the same as, larger than, or smaller than the strawman base. I'll refer to the base as B-star.

Take a look at Figure 1.

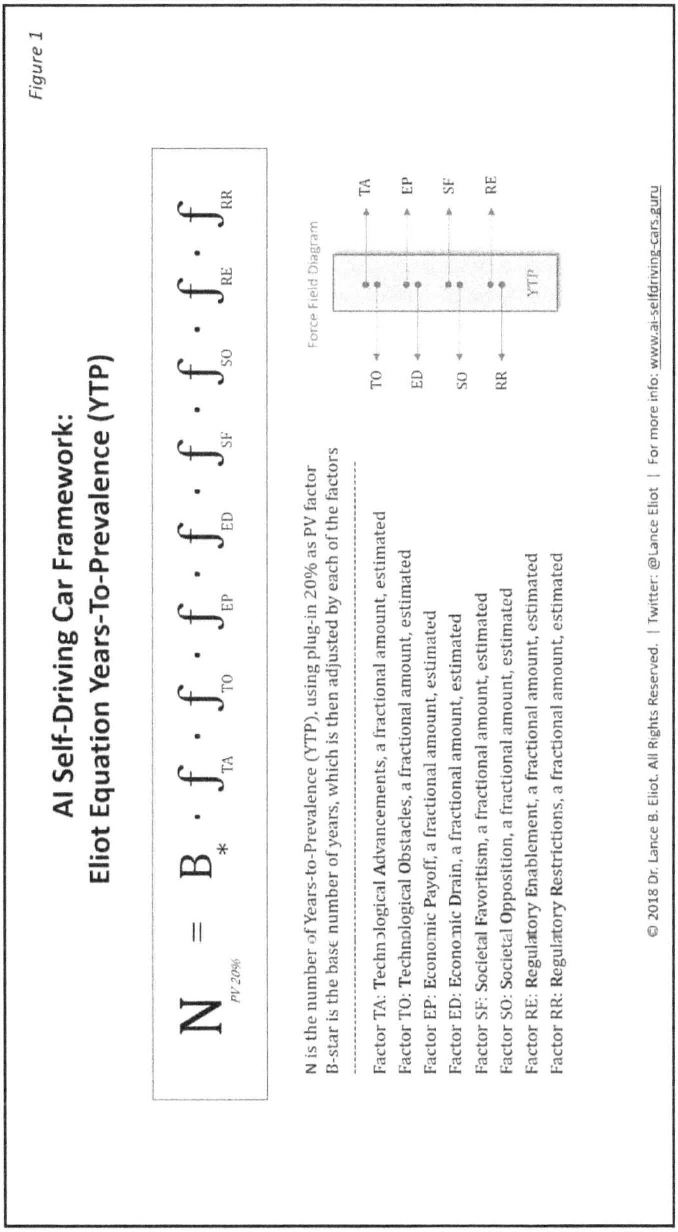
Figure 1
AI Self-Driving Car Framework:
Eliot Equation Years-To-Prevalence (YTP)
$N_{PV\ 20\%} = B_* \cdot f_{TA} \cdot f_{TO} \cdot f_{EP} \cdot f_{ED} \cdot f_{SF} \cdot f_{SO} \cdot f_{RE} \cdot f_{RR}$
N is the number of Years-to-Prevalence (YTP), using plug-in 20% as PV factor
B-star is the base number of years, which is then adjusted by each of the factors
Factor TA: Technological Advancements, a fractional amount, estimated
Factor TO: Technological Obstacles, a fractional amount, estimated
Factor EP: Economic Payoff, a fractional amount, estimated
Factor ED: Economic Drain, a fractional amount, estimated
Factor SF: Societal Favoritism, a fractional amount, estimated
Factor SO: Societal Opposition, a fractional amount, estimated
Factor RE: Regulatory Enablement, a fractional amount, estimated
Factor RR: Regulatory Restrictions, a fractional amount, estimated
Force Field Diagram
TO
TA
ED
EP
SO
SF
RR
RE
YTP
© 2018 Dr. Lance B. Eliot. All Rights Reserved. | Twitter: @Lance Eliot | For more info: www.ai-selfdriving-cars.guru

We are trying to solve for N. There is the base B-star which is then multiplied by eight factors.

For definitional purposes:

- N is the number of Years-to-Prevalence (YTP), using plug-in 20% as a PV (Prevalence) factor
- B-star is the base number of years, which is then adjusted by each of the factors

The key factors consist of:

- Factor TA: **T**echnological **A**dvancements, a fractional amount, estimated
- Factor TO: **T**echnological **O**bstacles, a fractional amount, estimated
- Factor EP: **E**conomic **P**ayoff, a fractional amount, estimated
- Factor ED: **E**conomic **D**rain, a fractional amount, estimated
- Factor SF: **S**ocietal **F**avoritism, a fractional amount, estimated
- Factor SO: **S**ocietal **O**pposition, a fractional amount, estimated
- Factor RE: **R**egulatory **E**nablement, a fractional amount, estimated
- Factor RR: **R**egulatory **R**estrictions, a fractional amount, estimated

The equation consists of this:

- N (PV of 20%) = B-star x TA x TO x EP x ED x SF x SO x RE x RR

Next, take a look at Figure 2.

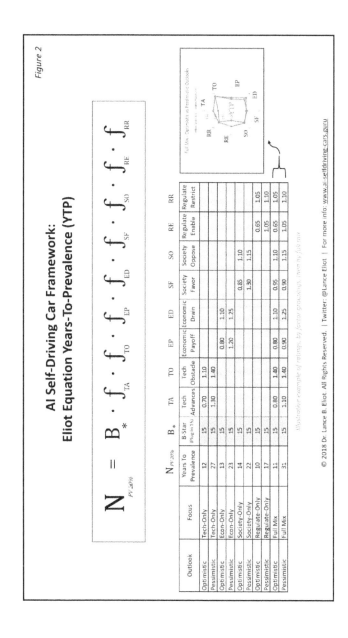

Figure 2

As per my earlier discussion, there are four overarching factors involving technology, economic, societal, and regulatory matters.

For each factor, there is the push-pull, meaning that each factor can be construed as an element that will foster and push along the advent of AI self-driving cars, and there is also a companion factor that is the pull that yanks away from the advent of AI self-driving cars. That's then four key factors which is doubled to account for the push-pull effect, arriving at 8 key factors.

Similar to the earlier remarks about the usability of equations, I've kept this equation to 9 elements, which is on par with the popular magical number seven plus or minus two rule-of-thumb. The factors are all readily comprehendible. The equation is readily comprehensible.

It is not intended to be the end-all be-all. It is intended to provide a kind of anchor around which discussion and debate can take place. Without having an anchor, arguments and discussions on this matter are often vacuous and roundabout.

As shown in Figure 2, I've populated a spreadsheet to make use of the equation.

At first, I've opted to show what might happen if you were to consider a solo-factor only perspective. For example, you might be using solely a technologist's perspective and so those factors are the only ones populated (the rest are assumed to drop out of the equation, rather than being say the value of zero, which would of course wipe out the calculations). Likewise, I show a solo-economic perspective, and then a solo-societal perspective, and a solo-regulatory perspective.

In the last two rows of the spreadsheet, I provide a full mix.

I've also opted to show an optimist's viewpoint and a pessimist's viewpoint, doing so for each of the solo-factor instances and for the full mix instance. This is in keeping with trying to arrive at a range of values, rather than a singleton value. The optimistic view and the pessimistic view provide an estimated lower bound and an estimated upper bound, respectively.

For the base B-star, the question arises as to what number to use for it. Since there are many pundits that seem to be floating around the number of 15 years, I've used that in this illustrative example. We could use 5 years, 10 years, 20 years, 25 years, or 30 years, all of which have been bandied around in the media. Presumably, whichever base you choose, the factors should ultimately "correct" it to tend toward whatever the "actual" prediction will be.

We are in the midst of carrying out a Delphi method approach to arrive at substantive lower and upper bounds. The Delphi method is a well-established forecasting method, often referred to as ETE (Estimate-Talk-Estimate). In this case, a set of experts in the field of AI self-driving cars have been canvased to participate in a series of Delphi rounds. With each round, the selected experts can see the indications of the other experts and adjust their own estimates as they deem appropriate to do so.

Though the Delphi method is generally held in high regard, it can be criticized for its potential of groupthink and can at times be weakened by excessive consensus. Nonetheless, it is instructive, and another means to spark useful discussion about the topic.

Conclusion

When will there be an advent of AI self-driving cars? Some answer this question by amorphous hunches. Via the use of the proposed herein equation, it is hoped that a more tangible and structured discussion and debate can take place.

You might not like the factors used, or you might want to add additional factors, but at least either way this equation gets the tree planted. From these roots will expectantly spring a widely sophisticated undertaking on the advent question.

Some critics of AI self-driving cars have said that we'll never have a true AI self-driving car. If that's the case, I guess the number for N is either zero (which we'll define as meaning it will never happen) or maybe infinite. I suppose I'm more optimistic and would like to assert that there is a number for N, which is not zero and nor infinite, and more akin to a value less than one hundred, and likely less than 50.

I've already stated that the Gen Z will be the generation that determines the advent of AI self-driving cars, which I still believe to be the case.

Equations, we love them, and we at times hate them (such as when memorizing them for taking tests or quizzes). Take a look at my proposed equation and see what you think. Plug-in some values. Mull over what might occur in the future. Though not a crystal ball, it is a kind of playbook of how to think about the future and the emergence of true AI self-driving cars.

MODULAR AUTONOMOUS SYSTEMS
AND
AI SELF-DRIVING CARS

CHAPTER 4
MODULAR AUTONOMOUS SYSTEMS AND AI SELF-DRIVING CARS

Eli Whitney is well-known for his invention of the cotton gin and for using the budding approach of interchangeable parts to produce his ingenious device. Until the emergence of interchangeable parts as a means of production, most devices and systems were typically crafted by-hand and varied significantly in terms of the size and the fitting of the various parts involved. Variations in size and fit meant that key elements could not just be snapped together, and nor could you readily do repairs and replacements since it required idiosyncratic by-hand one-off manufacturing.

You might not be aware that Eli Whitney was actually more successful at applying the interchangeable parts approach to the making of guns. In the case of the cotton gin, he ultimately made very little money from the remarkable invention, mainly due to those that openly violated his patent and copied his same designs, doing so en masse and his lawsuits were generally unable to stop the stealing of his approach. Nonetheless, he started a wave toward interchangeable parts as a prudent and successful form of production. We can all be thankful for that impetus.

Eli leveraged his notoriety of the cotton gin to win a massive federal government contract to make 10,000 muskets in preparation for the United States going to war with France. He vowed that he could produce the unheard-of volume by exploiting the interchangeable parts approach and won the contract by claiming he could get the project done in less than two years. Most doubted the possibility of his doing so.

The doubters turned out to be right and after two years had passed, he was still desperately trying to put together his production line and do so with the interchangeable parts method of building and assembly. Congress along with incoming president Thomas Jefferson and outgoing president John Adams demanded to know what Eli was doing and wanted to know when the government would receive its sorely needed muskets. Apparently, Eli went to Washington D.C. and did quite an act of showmanship to buy himself more time.

Standing in front of an assembled group of top dignitaries that included the two presidents, Eli supposedly laid out an array of musket parts, strewn on top of a large table top. He then proceeded to seemingly randomly select a part, and then randomly select another part into which it was to fit, and readily plugged them together. The crowd was stunned and elated.

Keep in mind that when making a musket at this time period in history, each part would be handcrafted and have to be shaped to fit properly to another also handcrafted part. This would take many hours to do and be extremely laborious. Plus, no two such parts could be used on another musket per se, unless you handcrafted them over again. Eli's bold demonstration that you could just pick-up any one of the parts and snap them together was unfathomable to most and was as impressive as any breathtaking magic trick, such as pulling a rabbit out of a hat or making an elephant disappear on a stage.

As a result of the vivid demonstration, he kept the massive contract and he gained even more federal work.

Some allege that he pulled a fast one on the onlookers and had actually discretely marked the parts beforehand, allowing him to know which ones would actually fit to which other ones. Notably, it was he that actually "randomly" selected the parts from the table and not someone else, thus, presumably, it was possible to appear as though just any part would fit with any other part. Devious? Contrived? Or simply a good magician. You decide.

In any case, Thomas Jefferson was later to credit the dawning of the machine age to Eli Whitney. Though Eli took several more years to produce the ordered muskets, they were considered of greater quality and more readily serviceable due to the interchangeable parts method. And, after finally getting his production line into shape, a subsequent order of 15,000 additional muskets was completed in record time and at a lower cost than if they had been made via the traditional individually handcrafted methods.

We now know that interchangeable parts is crucial to any kind of mass production. Sure, it might take longer to get your ducks aligned, having to design the parts to fit properly and devise a production line and manufacturing effort to achieve the needed precision, but in the end, you'll be able to more cheaply make the product. Not only is the cost ultimately lower per finished device or system, you can churn them out faster, and for maintenance and repairs the cost and effort is lessened.

There are circumstances whereby aiming to leverage an interchangeable parts approach might not be savvy. It's not a cure-all. If the number of needed units is low, or if the amount of time allowed to make the units is low, you might be better off jumping into the handcrafted method instead. There is a lot of overhead in making use of an interchangeable parts approach and therefore you need to ascertain for any given circumstance what the appropriate and most beneficial method is to be used.

A close brethen of interchangeable parts is the concept of modularization.

It makes sense to structure or architect your device or system into a series of modules when you are considering using an interchangeable parts approach. By decomposing something into various components or modules, you then can devise them so that they fit together well. Thus, you can then mass produce these smaller components or modules, and when piecing the whole thing together they will by-design snap together.

Modularity has other handy benefits too, beyond the notion of mass production. Presumably, you can focus on getting each module right, in a divide-and-conquer way, rather than having to try and get the entire system right all at once. Also, when things go awry, you can hopefully narrow down more readily where the problem lies, since you can progressively rule-in and rule-out the modules until you find the culprit within a particular module that is causing the problem.

In the software field, any software engineer worth their salt knows that modularity is vital to developing software. This is especially the case when the software is large-scale in size. The odds are that you'll have a team or many teams of software developers working on the system and trying to do so with one massive monolith is bound to be problematic. Instead, by architecting the system into modules, you can parcel out the effort to various teams or sub-teams and bring the system together as a whole when needed to do a wholescale system test of the numerous units or modules.

The development of AI systems is likewise usually benefited by structuring the system into modules. You are bound to have parts of the AI system that are leveraging AI techniques and capabilities, meanwhile there are likely other parts that are more conventional in their approach. You can architect the overall system into those modules that are AI specific and those that are more conventional. Of course, you don't need to modularize the system on that basis and might do so for other purposes such as based on functionality or other uses.

If you did subdivide an AI system into two overarching halves or layers, consisting of a half that had the AI and the other half that had more traditional elements, it would be a type of cleaving that might be handy. Presumably, at a later date, you might discover newer AI techniques and could then focus on embodying those into the AI half, possibly being able to leave the traditional element layer untouched. You might also want to port the system over to another platform, and if the half with the more traditional elements was handling those aspects, you could potentially switch out the traditional elements as a module and possibly not need to upset or change the AI layer.

Let's consider for a moment how the concepts of interchangeable parts and of modularization are related to cars.

By-and-large most automobiles are devised of interchangeable parts. You might have an engine that is one overall module and it contains a multitude of parts, all of which are made in an interchangeable way, allowing you to assemble an engine by snapping in the appropriate parts in the appropriate places.

The engine is likely able to be popped into the rest of the car and allow you to make the engines without having to do so as tailored to the particular car body and other car elements. It is all modularly devised and done so with interchangeable aspects, meaning too that you need to upfront get everything well figured out so they will fit together without difficulty.

At times, cars are devised into Knock-Down kits (referred to as KD).

The Knock-Down approach involves making some of the parts in one place and then shipping them to another place for final assembly. For example, you might make some of the parts in one country, export them to another country, and complete the assembly of the car in that other country.

Auto makers do this for several reasons including at times the benefit of possibly having some parts made at a lesser cost in another country and then bringing those parts to say the country in which the final assembly and then selling of the car will take place (there are often tax and financial benefits of doing things this way).

There are variants of the Knock-Down tactic. You can have all of the non-assembled parts in totality and ship those to a location to be assembled, in which case this is referred to as a Complete Knock-Down (CKD). If you have just part of the assembly, it is known as a Semi-Knocked-Down (SKD). When you are going to ship the Knock-Down to another country, this is known as a Knocked-Down Export (KDX). For the case of making the parts and assembling them into a whole car, doing so within the country of origin and then shipping them out to be sold, it is known as a Built-Up Export (BUX).

I'm guessing that most of us realize that the modularization of cars makes a lot of sense and have become accustomed to the notion. There is a slew of benefits by leveraging modularization. One aspect that might be surprising to you involves a form of modularization that you might not have yet explicitly considered, which I'll tell you about in a moment.

Remember how I earlier suggested that for an AI system we might modularize it into at least two major halves or layers, consisting of a layer that has the AI components and a second layer with the more traditional components. I'm not saying you need to do things that way, and only pointing it out as a possibility, which might or might not make sense depending upon the nature of the AI system that you are creating. Also, be clear that the modularization exists within those halves too, and thus I am not somehow suggesting that there are merely two monoliths, and instead saying that you could have a major modularization at the topmost level and then have modularization within those subsequent layers or modules.

For cars, suppose we tried to employ the same idea of dividing a car into two major halves or layers. If so, what would those layers consist of?

I suppose you could liken this to those magic acts that appear to split a person in half. Yikes, people weren't made to be split in half. It defies logic. We all know that the human body is built as one monolith and you cannot just cut it in half, though magicians try to make us believe otherwise. When a magician does this trick, do they cut the person in half lengthwise or by widthwise? Well, usually they cut the person around the stomach and have an upper and lower half (I've not seen magicians that try to cut a person down the middle of their length, which might be interesting to see, or perhaps disgusting to see).

In the case of a car, the seemingly most logical way to cut it into half would be to devise a lower half and an upper half. We'll refer to the lower half as the chassis of the car, which can also be referred to in many other ways, including calling it the platform, the undercarriage, the powertrain, the skateboard, and so on. The upper half we'll refer to as the body, or the body type, or some like to say it is a pod.

Let's then say that we're going to design a car that has two major halves, a lower half that is the chassis or platform, and an upper half that is the body or pod.

Why would we do this?

As long as we adhere to the interchangeable parts mantra, in theory we can make the chassis or platform in one place and later on attach the body or pod in another place. This would allow us to make the two halves in different parts of a country or in different countries, and yet still be able to bring them readily together when we wanted to do the final assembly.

This though is merely the advantage of production. We can also gain the advantage of possibly being able to reuse the chassis or platform and have a variety of body types or pods that we can place onto the chassis. This means that we can more likely have a multitude of different cars, which are hopefully easier to produce, by having our own "standardized" chassis or platform and then making a variety of pods that would be plopped onto the platform or chassis.

Pretend that you wanted to make a car that was primarily to be used for transporting people. You would want the interior of the car to be well-suited for people to be present in the car. There need to be seats that can accommodate the passengers. There needs to be protective gear such as air bags to provide safety aspects for the occupants. We might want to include in-car entertainment such as radios or TVs, and so on.

Suppose you also wanted to make a car that was primarily going to be used to transport goods. In that case, you don't need and nor want those seats that would be used in a passenger-oriented car. The seats are just going to get in the way of being able to stack boxes or items into the car. You don't need the entertainment gear since the boxes or bulky other items don't care about being entertained. You might want to have various straps and other restraints that would keep the goods from rolling around. And so on.

You would most likely construe that these differing needs would mean that we need to have two completely different cars. One car is designed and built as a passenger car. The other car is designed and built as a goods transport car. Two different purposes. Two different designs. Seemingly the only thing they have in-common is that they are both cars.

But, wait! If a chassis or platform contained all of the engine, tires, transmission, and other such "car mobility" elements, we need to realize that the aspects about the body or pod portion is where the differences are. The lower layer can be possibly the same, while it is just the upper layer that we want to change out.

Thus, rather than making two completely different cars, suppose we considered making a lower half or layer that was the mobility portion, and the upper half was the body type or pod. We could then aim to make a variety of upper halves that could plug into our "standardized" lower layer. Doing so would give us a great deal of flexibility.

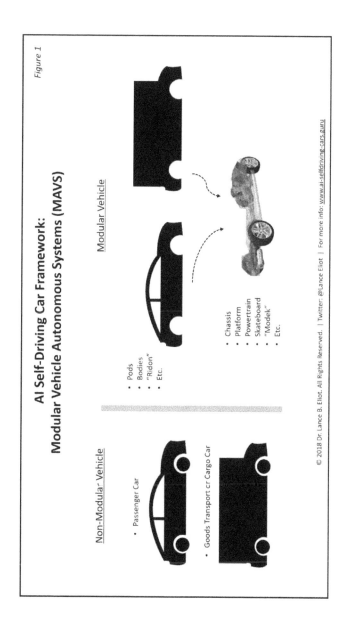

The flexibility of having a lower layer and a changeable upper layer could be quite attractive.

When making cars, it is tough to predict how many cars you are going to likely sell. If you guess wrong, you can end-up not having enough cars to meet the market demand, or you might end-up with an excess of cars and have a bloated and costly inventory leftover.

You might have an especially difficult time trying to determine how many passenger cars to make versus how many goods transport cars to make.

Also, a buyer of your passenger car or your transport car is usually locked into whichever choice they made when buying the car. I own a traditional passenger car and at times when I've helped my kids move to their apartments or dorms for college, I've tried to use my passenger car to haul their stuff, though this is not easy to do, such as fitting a large-screen TV or a surfboard into my passenger sized and shaped car.

Ideally, it would be nifty to buy a car that could transform from being a passenger car into a goods transport car or being a transporting of goods car to becoming a passenger car. We've seen the auto makers struggle mightily with this same aspect, doing so by making the seats in a passenger car be able to be pulled out or potentially lay flat. Likewise, they make SUV's or vans that can transport goods and that have collapsing seats or similar aspects to try and accommodate passengers.

Rather than trying to make one car that can do two things, we might instead consider making two cars that each does one thing well. The problem though is that we would normally need to make two different cars, which adds up in cost to produce and makes the prediction problem harder as to how many to make.

A solution might be to go ahead and make a chassis or platform that we can use universally for being the mobility center for whatever kinds of upper layers or pods that we might want to make. We could make one pod or upper layer that can superbly accommodate passengers. We could make another pod or upper layer that is well-suited to transporting goods. Etc.

This seems like a robust way to get the best of both worlds.

Of course, the catch consists of being able to actually be able to bring together the two halves and do so in a manner that is not overly arduous to achieve. If we are suggesting that you could readily switch from a passenger pod to a transport-of-goods pod, this implies that it is relatively easy to unplug one pod and plug in another pod.

Making a plug-and-play of an entire chassis with an entire pod, it's a challenge. You could liken this somewhat to playing with Legos, though these are rather large Legos and have a lot that would bind them together. Presumably, the upper layer is going to want to tap into the functions of the lower layer, such as getting electrical power, as a minimum, along with sharing of a multitude of other aspects.

This concept of having a lower layer of the car and an upper layer is often referred to as a modular vehicle. Auto industry insiders might refer to this as the Ridek, which I'll explain next.

A patent was awarded in the year 2000 to Dr. Gordon Dower for his invention of a modular vehicle, which also was an EV (Electrical Vehicle). The lower layer contained the engine, transmission, and so on, and he referred to it as the Modek, signifying the motorized or mobility layer (aka the chassis or platform). The upper layer was the Ridon. When you put together the Ridon with a Modek you got yourself a Ridek, the then usable car as a whole. General Motors (GM) came along in 2004 and attempted to patent a modular vehicle which they called the Autonomy. This led to a dispute about the matter.

When I attended this year's Consumer Electronics Show (CES) in January, the modular vehicle approach was a bit of a splash since Mercedes-Benz was unveiling their Urbanetic, a concept car based on the lower layer and upper layer approach. The pod or upper layer for passengers would accommodate about a dozen occupants. There would be windows, a moonroof, and LED displays, all of which would befit the needs of human passengers. A pod for transporting goods, considered a cargo module, would have around 350 cubic feet of space and could accommodate perhaps ten pallets or so of goods.

I more recently participated in the Autonomous Vehicles 2019 (AV19) Silicon Valley summit in February, and had a chance to speak with Mark Crawford, Chief Engineer at the Great Wall Motors Company. He shared with me and the attendees a glimpse at how they too are pursuing a modular vehicle approach, jam packed with AI and autonomous capabilities.

Those of you that follow the automotive industry are likely aware of the rise of the Great Wall Motors Company, a Chinese automobile maker. They are the biggest producer of SUV's for China and made a noteworthy accomplishment in 2016 when they passed the one million mark of cars sold in that year. Being in business since 1984, the auto maker is a household name in China, and gradually becoming known in other countries. In case you are wondering about the name of the firm, they opted to leverage the popular Great Wall of China moniker for the firm's name.

This all brings me to the topic of MAVS.

Modular Autonomous Vehicle Systems (MAVS) is an up-and-coming buzzword and approach that consists of devising a lower half or chassis/platform upon which you can then interchangeably place a body type or pod, plus infusing autonomous capabilities into the resultant car. It's a fascinating notion and one that is worth further analysis – I'll do so in a moment.

What does this have to do with AI self-driving cars?

At the Cybernetic AI Self-Driving Car Institute, we are developing AI software for self-driving cars. The MAVS is a variation of AI self-driving cars and can impact the nature of AI self-driving cars and their advent. It's worth knowing about and being included into your thinking about the future of AI self-driving cars.

Allow me to elaborate.

I'd like to first clarify and introduce the notion that there are varying levels of AI self-driving cars. The topmost level is considered Level 5. A Level 5 self-driving car is one that is being driven by the AI and there is no human driver involved. For the design of Level 5 self-driving cars, the auto makers are even removing the gas pedal, brake pedal, and steering wheel, since those are contraptions used by human drivers. The Level 5 self-driving car is not being driven by a human and nor is there an expectation that a human driver will be present in the self-driving car. It's all on the shoulders of the AI to drive the car.

For self-driving cars less than a Level 5, there must be a human driver present in the car. The human driver is currently considered the responsible party for the acts of the car. The AI and the human driver are co-sharing the driving task. In spite of this co-sharing, the human is supposed to remain fully immersed into the driving task and be ready at all times to perform the driving task. I've repeatedly warned about the dangers of this co-sharing arrangement and predicted it will produce many untoward results.

Let's focus herein on the true Level 5 self-driving car. Much of the comments apply to the less than Level 5 self-driving cars too, but the fully autonomous AI self-driving car will receive the most attention in this discussion.

Here's the usual steps involved in the AI driving task:

- Sensor data collection and interpretation
- Sensor fusion
- Virtual world model updating
- AI action planning
- Car controls command issuance

Another key aspect of AI self-driving cars is that they will be driving on our roadways in the midst of human driven cars too. There are some pundits of AI self-driving cars that continually refer to a utopian world in which there are only AI self-driving cars on the public roads. Currently there are about 250+ million conventional cars in the United States alone, and those cars are not going to magically disappear or become true Level 5 AI self-driving cars overnight.

Indeed, the use of human driven cars will last for many years, likely many decades, and the advent of AI self-driving cars will occur while there are still human driven cars on the roads. This is a crucial point since this means that the AI of self-driving cars needs to be able to contend with not just other AI self-driving cars, but also contend with human driven cars. It is easy to envision a simplistic and rather unrealistic world in which all AI self-driving cars are politely interacting with each other and being civil about roadway interactions. That's not what is going to be happening for the foreseeable future. AI self-driving cars and human driven cars will need to be able to cope with each other. Period.

Returning to the topic of Modular Autonomous Vehicles Systems or MAVS, let's consider how this relates to AI self-driving cars.

First, one of the most essential questions facing any tech firm or auto maker that wants to develop an AI system for purposes of imbuing a self-driving car is whether to use an existing conventional car as your base or opt to craft something anew.

You might recall that in the earlier days of AI self-driving car efforts there was a tendency toward crafting a new kind of car that would house the AI system. Waymo's initial efforts went in this direction, and it was long rumored that Apple was aiming to do likewise (as were many other of the auto makers and tech firms in this space).

The logic at the time was that you might as well own and be able to fully control the entire car, soup to nuts, as they say, rather than trying to leverage an existing automobile that you likely otherwise had less control over.

There was also perhaps a bit of bravado involved, sparked by the assumption that it would be nifty to have your own branded car. In that case, you could sell the entire self-driving car, along with the bundled AI system for the autonomous elements. Why have to share the revenue and profits with some established car maker when you could do the whole enchilada. Mixed into the business sensibility was a brazen belief that making a car was relatively easy to do.

Some of this brashness was also due to the origins of many of the self-driving car efforts, namely arising from academic and university settings. In such an environment, you often piece together your own prototype, at times entirely from scratch. This led many of the AI developers that shifted into industry to assume they would do likewise at the auto maker or tech firm that landed them.

The harsh reality is that making a car that can be mass produced, and which can withstand the rigors of daily use in the real-world, requires a lot more effort and knowledge than it does to make a prototype in a research lab. Trying to scale-up a prototype to meet all of the regulatory requirements of an actual public roadway allowed car is daunting. Figuring out how to mass produce a car and make money doing so, well, that wasn't in the wheelhouse of many AI developers.

One concern too was that you would be splitting your limited attention and resources toward trying to solve two different problems at the same time.

You are trying to develop and field the AI autonomous systems aspects, which of itself is absolutely a moonshot regarding trying to get to a Level 5 true AI self-driving car. Meanwhile, if you are also involved in designing and making the car itself, this becomes a huge distraction from the AI side of things. When I say distraction, don't misconstrue this to imply that making the car itself is inconsequential, in fact it is immensely consequential.

Think about it this way. If you craft some tremendous AI system, but the underlying car stinks, you aren't likely to get very far along on achieving true AI self-driving cars. A car that cannot run or falters constantly is not much of a solid base to use for the AI aspects. Indeed, I would assert that few would realize that your AI self-driving car was anything wonderous if it was continually breaking down, presumably due to the car aspects of the self-driving car.

That also brings up another difficulty about trying to solve two problems at once. If you did decide to make your own new car, when things go awry, how can you discern whether the problem exists in the arena of the car versus in the arena of the AI system. It would be overly complicated to do so. Things would be simpler if you knew that the car was essentially "perfected" and workable, allowing you to generally rule out issues being in the car arena and instead focus on the AI system.

For a slew of such reasons, most of the tech firms have banded together with auto makers that make cars. Or, you could look at it the other way too, encompassing that the auto makers opted to band together with the tech firms that do the AI systems. Furthermore, they generally are using a base of an existing "perfected" car to build the AI into and onto, such as Waymo's use of the Chrysler Pacifica minivan for their Arizona tryouts.

Ideally, the AI systems aspects can be ported over to other models of cars, though this has yet to be seen as a readily possible aspect. Right now, the goal is pretty much to get a car working that has the possibility of becoming a true AI self-driving car, and whatever you choose as the base for now is fine. You can worry about the reusability once you've gotten the AI systems to work as intended.

I don't want to leave you with the impression that the base car can be anything that you willy-nilly choose. As mentioned, the base car should at least be something that works and has a track record of working. The next variant would be a newer model of an existing car that works, such that the new changes are mild enough that you can expect the newer model will overall work too. A brand-new car that has never seen the roadways is potentially more problematic.

When I say this, I know that some tech firms and auto makers would argue that they would rather start fresh and redesign a car to be suitable for AI self-driving car purposes. Yes, that's a certainly attractive approach. We already know and acknowledge that true AI self-driving cars will have quite different interiors, since there won't be a need for a human driver's position anymore.

In that case, if you are building upon any existing car, one that is being sold to be used on our roadways today, there is obviously going to be an entire setup for a human driver. It's only the concept cars that showcase the lack of a driver's position. It makes little sense today to mass produce a car that has no human driving capacity, since who would buy it? Pretty much nobody, since the car would be little more than a lofty looking paperweight.

It is a bit of a conundrum. We want to eventually all excise out the human driver, which then will allow for the interior of the self-driving car to be completely envisioned. For now, this is not particularly practical since we don't yet have anything that is able to drive like a true AI self-driving system, thus, a car either needs to allow for a human driver or be potentially sold purely as a human driven car, it's a matter or practicality.

Logically, you might as well aim at a conventional car that has the human driver position, allowing you to anyway workout the AI side of things, along with having a human back-up driver present in the car. Once you've got that running well, it should be relatively straightforward to port over to a specially designed new kind of car that is shaped and built for self-driving purposes.

In that case, you've now fortunately kept the situation to one problem rather than trying to solve two problems at once. In theory, you've gotten the AI system to work well and thus you won't need to overly focus on it, and meanwhile the focus goes toward the new kind of car and making sure it works. I don't want to imply that the porting is going to be easy. It can be very hard, depending upon how the original AI system was devised.

For some AI developers, if they aren't structuring their software in a modular fashion, it is going to be a devil of a time to port their AI system over to some other kind of car. The odds are that their monolith AI has a ton of embedded assumptions about the underlying car that was originally used. Finding those assumptions will be like finding a needle in a haystack.

Whether the AI developers were able to think ahead and get ready for a future of porting their AI would be partially based on not just their own skills, but also on the auto maker or tech firm itself. If the auto maker or tech firm is in a pell-mell rush to be the first to achieve a true AI self-driving car, they might apply such immense pressure to the AI development efforts that anything that seems to cause a delay or inhibit progress gets tossed aside. AI developers that might have wanted to take a more modular approach could be overruled and told to just make things work. Being first might be considered a high priority than having something that is portable. As they say, there is little or no style when you are immersed in a street fight.

I'm not suggesting that the strive to be first is mistaken. It could be that the first to succeed gets all the glory and might capture the market, in which case they can deal with the porting aspects later on. The first such true AI self-driving cars are likely to gain huge acclaim and attention. The headlines will herald as heroes the auto maker and tech firm that managed to achieve the vaunted goal.

Generally, few though tend to believe that being first is an applicable first-mover's advantage in the case of AI self-driving cars. There are many instances in the tech field of those getting to a new technology first that ultimately were not the "winners" and found themselves eclipsed by those that came along after them.

Some claim that the first true AI self-driving car maker is actually going to likely be the one that gets the most arrows in their back, presumably since their AI self-driving car has gotten into untoward circumstances while attempting to get it market ready. The heat and tarnished reputation might put their AI self-driving car into an early grave, and meanwhile some other upstart provides the same capability but has escaped the gauntlet of reputation smashing that the first-move undertook.

I've dragged you somewhat laboriously through the question of whether to use an existing car or whether to aim at a brand-new car as your base for developing the AI system for a self-driving car.

Let's try to look at the question in a different light. I'm going to tie things back to the topic of modular vehicles.

Rather than making an AI self-driving car by using a whole car, suppose instead you focused on a modular vehicle, specifically a car that is divided into a lower half for the chassis or platform and had a top layer for the pod or body type.

One approach would be to cram all of the AI self-driving car elements into the lower layer. In this manner, you could then mix-and-match other top layers of pods. Those pods would not presumably need any kind of AI capability per se, in terms of the mobility for the self-driving car. This makes it simpler to make different kinds of pods.

This approach assumes that you can have the AI self-driving car capabilities self-contained into the chassis. Maybe this is feasible, maybe not.

For example, let's assume you are going to use radar, LIDAR, ultrasonic sensors, cameras and the like, all part of the sensory apparatus needed to enable the self-driving car and the AI to navigate and analyze the environment around the self-driving car. Where will those sensors be?

If you put all of those sensors solely into the chassis, this might be problematic. The LIDAR usually needs to be on top of the entire vehicle and be given a 360-degree unimpeded ability to scan the environment. Many of the other sensors are likewise most effective when placed at a position higher up on a vehicle. Would you be able to do this if the sensors were all contained solely within the chassis?

As such, you might have little choice other than to split the AI system across both the chassis and the pod. You might be able to put most of the guts of the AI system into the chassis, and then have the so-called peripheral devices like some of the sensors built into the pod. Some of the sensors might reside in the chassis and some of the sensors would reside in the pod.

In that case, you need to ensure that all of the pods have those sensory devices baked into them. You also need to make sure that however you connect the chassis and the respective pod will allow for the interfacing of the sensors that are on the pod with the guts of the AI system that resides in the chassis. One possible downside would be any latency introduced by using that connecting interface. Though, you could make the same argument about even a conventional car that has an "integrated" AI system, meaning that how the sensors are interconnected might suffer a similar kind of latency.

Take a look at Figure 2.

Figure 2

AI Self-Driving Car Framework:
Modular Vehicle Autonomous Systems (MAVS)

Classifications of Autonomous Use

	Conventional Modular	Autonomous Chassis	Autonomous Pod	Autonomous Dual Lite	Autonomous Full-Lite	Autonomous Lite-Full	Autonomous Full-Full
Chassis	No AV	AV (full)	No AV	AV Lite	AV Full	AV Lite	AV Full
Pods	No AV	No AV	AV (full)	AV Lite	AV Lite	AV Full	AV Full
Acronym	CMV	MAC	MAP	MAD-L	MAV-FL	MAV-LF	MAD-F

Can the chassis by itself roll around and act like a self-driving car?

It depends once again on the nature of the sensors and where those sensors are placed. If some of the sensors are going to be contained in the pods, the chassis is essentially blind without having a mated pod. It could be that the chassis has sufficient sensors to be able to move around to some lesser degree, and not be able to fully travel on conventional roads without having a properly mated pod.

Speaking about the pods, we would now have the handy aspect that we could have one kind of pod that accommodates human passengers, and have a different pod that accommodates goods transportation. This does away with the earlier problem of trying to make one car that can do two different things. We now have a self-driving car that could be outfitted with the passenger pod for purposes of doing say ridesharing and being re-outfitted with the cargo carrying pod when you wanted the AI self-driving car to transport goods.

The nature of the removal or disconnecting of the pods, along with the coupling or adding on of the pods to the chassis will be crucial in this setup. Suppose you own a fleet of AI self-driving cars. During the day you might want 90% of them to be outfitted for passenger use. Late at night, you instead want to use 70% of them for cargo carrying and keep just 30% in a mode for passenger purposes. This means that at some point during a day, you will bring the fleet to a warehouse or some kind of location that has your pods, and you'll want to make the switchovers there.

If it takes hours to make the switchover of each AI self-driving car, you'll be in a quandary. Is it better to lose the potential revenue of those AI self-driving cars doing their ridesharing in order to "waste" the presumably no-income time of the switchover, in hopes that the money you'll make for those AI self-driving cars as cargo carriers will be sufficient? Plus, you'll need in the morning to do the switchover once again.

This kind of switching is only going to make dollars-and-sense if the switch over is relatively fast and easy to do. If the switchover is long to do, that's a downside. If the switchover is complicated, that's a downside in that you might have heightened costs involved in just doing the switchover. We need to also consider whether the switchover can be botched, namely that in the act of switching pods, it might be overly easy to damage either the chassis or the pod, thus undermining the potential ROI (Return on Investment) and having to continually replace or repair those chassis and pods.

On the topic of safety, it will be crucial too how the pods are attached to the chassis.

Suppose the AI self-driving car is zipping along on an autobahn at over 100 miles per hour. The AI detects debris up ahead. To avoid the debris, the AI commands the self-driving car to make a radical swerving motion. There is cargo inside the pod, rather than humans, and so the AI is able to make a more radical maneuver, realizing that it is merely cargo and not going to impact any humans that otherwise could not withstand the G-forces involved.

Will the attached pod be securely enough fashioned to handle this maneuver? If not, the pod might slide off the chassis, which obviously would be detrimental, or it might go askew, which is not a desirable status. In a conventional car that is not a modular vehicle, you presumably don't think about the chances that the top part of the car is going to unexpectedly come off the bottom part of the car.

This brings up some notable aspects about the Machine Learning or Deep Learning that might be different when aiming at a Modular Autonomous Vehicle System. Do you train the Machine Learning or Deep Learning on a particular kind of pod, such as the passenger pod, and then it is instantiated when that pod is placed onto the chassis, and do likewise separately for the cargo pod, or do you mesh together the Machine Learning and Deep Learning for both types of pods?

I mention this because of my example about the AI self-driving car on the autobahn.

Recall that I said the AI knew that the cargo pod was being used and could therefore make more radical maneuvers. The Machine Learning or Deep Learning might or might not have realized that those differing pods can allow the AI to treat the driving task differently. AI developers might need to explicitly establish differing conditions and aspects to make sure that the Machine Learning or Deep Learning is "aware" that the self-driving car is going to be able to act differently depending upon the pod that is attached.

Indeed, I would argue that the entire AI system of the self-driving car would need to be architected toward the notion that there are going to be different kinds of pods being used. I've so far only mentioned two types of pods, one for passengers and one for transporting goods. There are likely going to be other kinds of pods that we might devise. In each instance of a pod type, the AI will need to be somehow revised or retooled, along with doing the various testing and redeployment efforts.

When the Ridek was patented, it was envisioned that the buyers might rent the Modek (the chassis) and possibly buy the pod or Ridon. That's one way to do things. It could be the other way in that you opt to buy the chassis and rent the pod, allowing you to later on switch to a different kind of pod. Or, the entire setup of both the chassis and a pod is sold, perhaps even selling multiple pod types to someone that wants to have a complete set. It's a mix-and-match opportunity.

On a related note, suppose the chassis was made as a kind of "open source" that you could then create your own pods and use those on the chassis itself. This might allow for a multitude of varying kinds of pods. An entire ecosystem of pods might emerge. Of course, the auto maker or tech firm that made the original chassis is then taking a chance and assuming that those pods are going to be suitable for the chassis. If someone does a rotten pod and the chassis gets into an untoward situation, it could be like the bad apple in the barrel that spoils the whole bunch.

Shifting gears, let's briefly consider the matter of having a multitude of these MAVS and how they might work together as a team of virtualized ground-based mobility devices.

I've mentioned previously in my writing and speaking that we'll gradually be leveraging a kind of Swarm Intelligence (SI) by having interacting AI self-driving cars. This brings together advances in Distributed AI (sometimes abbreviated as either DAI or DI), along with the efforts of dealing with Multi-Robotic Systems (MRS). In the case of AI self-driving cars, assuming we can achieve individualized behaviors that are sufficient, the next step would be to have them working together in various ways.

For example, you might have them sharing roadway and infrastructure information with each other, allowing any single AI self-driving car to achieve what I call omnipresence. You might have the AI self-driving cars aiding each other in a pack or group manner. This could include a caravan of AI self-driving cars and/or the use of AI self-driving cars for platooning purposes.

Mark Crawford provided a grand vision of interacting MAVS that would collaborate with each other. This is the kind of visionary perspective that we need to be thinking about and I applaud him for his efforts in doing so.

I realize that for many of the auto makers and tech firms it is hard right now to be taking a macroscopic view when you are in the trenches and trying to get your AI self-driving cars to work. Ultimately, it is crucial that we begin identifying a future that we can layout, and be creating a path now to build toward that future. Let's not get ourselves painted into a corner by the AI systems we strive to build today. I'd like to hope and aim for architecting AI system for self-driving cars that will grow and mature and evolve as the advent of AI self-driving cars proceeds.

Conclusion

Should AI self-driving cars be divided into two halves like a magician does on stage? When you consider the nature of what a car is or does, it makes sense that you could divide it into two layers, unlike how humans themselves are made.

Dividing up a car into a lower layer and an upper layer might be handy twofer.

You can mix-and-match the bottom layer with a multitude of different use-case pods.

Though I didn't mention that you could potentially have differing chassis too, that's another possibility. You might have a workhorse chassis that is less nimble and slower, while you might have a chassis that is turbocharged and able to carry heavy loads or go at extremely fast speeds. This means that you have many choices of mixing varying kinds of chassis with varying kinds of pods.

To some degree, this dual layered approach enters into an unknown territory for cars.

We don't have today any mass production large-scale examples of cars that are built and sold in this manner. We do though have an enormous industry of trucks that haul a wide array of freight vehicles, including flatbed trailers, step deck trailers, refrigerated trailers, dry trailers, and so on. Thus, it is certainly well-established that having a mix-and-match capability can be prudent.

Modular vehicles are taking a step toward the future by becoming autonomous modular vehicles.

The AI systems that are being devised for AI self-driving cars can be architected for handling modular vehicles and bringing modular vehicles into the autonomous realm. These are exciting times and we'll all need to be keenly attentive to what kinds of AI self-driving cars come into the marketplace and which ones gain prevalence. AI might just make modular vehicles into a big triumph.

CHAPTER 5

DRIVER'S LICENSING AND AI SELF-DRIVING CARS

CHAPTER 5

DRIVER'S

LICENSING

AND

AI SELF-DRIVING CARS

Rites of passage. I

n some countries and locales, you need to hunt down a lion to undertake a rite of passage.

Here in California, it seems like our mainstay rite of passage is getting your driver's license or driver's permit. Up until getting a vaunted license to drive, you are considered somewhat inessential and possibly even an annoyance, since you need to either harangue someone to give you a lift or you need to find an alternative form of transportation other than a car.

For my children, it was exciting to see them earn their driver's permit. After years of chauffeuring them around, which was a delight to do and I miss it sorely, there was a great sense of pride that they could now drive a car.

Having a driver's license meant that they could pretty much go where they wanted and when they wanted, though subject to a personal curfew and a state-based curfew (legally, for the first twelve months, teens cannot drive after 11 p.m. and before 5 a.m., though exceptions such as for work are allowed).

Some teenagers complain about the gauntlet they need to confront when seeking to become a licensed driver. I'd heard scuttlebutt among some teenagers at my children's school that maybe there was a kind of conspiracy going on, in which adults were scheming to keep kids from driving cars. Rumors were that only a tiny percentage of teens that passed the licensing requirements would actually get anointed with a license.

I mulled over this theory and found out that by-and-large most teens do get their driver's licenses (assuming they take things seriously), and in terms of the licensing roadblocks trying to keep them from doing so, well, it sure seems prudent to make sure that anyone licensed to drive is properly qualified and ready to do so. That's not a conspiracy, that's just plain sensible, I'd say.

Historians believe that Karl Benz in 1888 was the first person to ever receive a driver's license. Just three years earlier, he had patented what some suggest was the first practical automobile, and after some complaints by those that were annoyed by the stink and smell of his motorcar that he personally drove around, the government decided to establish the need to first obtain a written permit to drive a car. He dutifully got his permit and continued to drive his Motorwagen. In case you are wondering, yes, Karl Benz is the same person as named in the now popular Mercedes Benz moniker.

Nearly twenty years later, the United States put in place a driver's licensing law that first took hold in New York. It was on August 1, 1910 that the first such licenses were granted, though it was only needed by professional drivers such as chauffeurs. A few years later, starting in 1913, New Jersey opted to force all drivers to become licensed and included the need to pass a mandatory test before you would be granted the license.

A driver's license has become more than just a signification that you are licensed to drive a car. As many college students can attest, having a driver's license is the key to survival when being a partying and bar hopping university student. No driver's license, no means to get that keg of beer for your frat or sorority. Or so it would seem, yet the reality is that there is a vast underground market of fake ID's that are readily available. In any case, the point is that a driver's license is often used as a form of identification, not necessarily solely for proof of being able to drive a car.

When you consider the act of driving a car, it becomes apparent that there are two major elements of certification about the matter. There is the aspect of ensuring that the human driver is ready, able, and formally certified to drive, which is achieved by the driver's license or permit, plus there is the need to make sure that the car itself is also properly certified.

You likely don't put much thought toward the fact that the car you are driving had to meet various federal regulatory guidelines in order to be on the public roadways. Per the Federal Motor Vehicle Safety Standards (FMVSS), all cars on our roads are supposed to satisfy a rather hefty number of federally mandated requirements. The requirements encompass the full scope of car elements, including the car design, the construction of the car, the performance of the car, it's safety, its durability, and so on.

Those brakes on your car, yep, they come under FMVSS standards number 106 and other provisions. Even something that might seem to be trivial, such as the windshield wipers, those too come under the FMVSS regulations (item number 104). There are various international standards and other countries also have their standards. If you are an auto maker, you face a rather long list of requirements that your car needs to meet, often times varying by country and forcing you to make some tough decisions about how you design and develop your car, along with whether it is worth the trouble to sell your car in places that might have regulations you aren't interested in meeting.

In the United States, we have chosen to use the federal government to certify cars, and in contrast chosen to have the states themselves certify the human drivers of those cars. Does it have to be that way? Nope. It's custom and tradition.

We could certainly decide to have the feds certify cars and certify drivers, doing both, if that's what we wanted to do as a society. The states though have historically held onto the driver certification aspects. You could assert that it makes sense to have the states certify drivers since each state also comes up with their own driving regulations. The tricky part is that the federal transportation laws regulate travel between the states and in the end, it has fortunately turned out that most states tend to have by-and-large similar regulations, easing the driving across the vast landscape of the United States.

If you are wondering whether perhaps states opt to regulate cars and also regulate drivers, the basis for having the feds regulate cars themselves is to again foster an across the United States ease of using your car. Imagine if every state had idiosyncratic rules about the design and make-up of a car. It could be a nightmare for you when taking a family trip that took you through numerous states. Upon entering each state, you might be violating some car regulation in that state and find yourself never making it across those states unimpeded.

There is also the case to be made that by having one entity, the federal government, regulating cars the matter is simplified for the auto makers (else they'd need to be negotiating endlessly and/or trying to comply with each of the 50 different states individually). One could also claim that there is an economy of scale to be had by embodying all of the car regulations into the hands of the federal government. The states seem to be generally satisfied with the arrangement and aren't necessarily going out of their way to try and change the status quo on that aspect.

Overall, it seems to be a pretty workable approach. The federal government certifies the cars that are allowed onto our roadways. The states certify the human drivers of those cars. I suppose it is the yin and yang of the arrangement.

Let's dig a bit more deeply into how the states tend to certify drivers.

I'm going to focus on the licensing of human drivers for conventional cars. I mention this point because there are other kinds of driver licensing needed to drive trucks, or buses, or to drive a motorcycle, and to drive other non-car types of vehicles.

Most of the driver's licensing requirements are about the same, though the type of vehicle can cause the driver licensing steps to differ, and some would say become more stringent too for when driving a bus or similar multi-person vehicle of a larger size (this seems sensible, since one could argue a bus is a more complicated vehicle and also one that holds the lives of a multitude of passengers at once).

There are about nine major steps when getting a driver's license. Again, keep in mind that the number of steps and their specific actions will differ by state. I've just tried to come up with the major steps and do so to generally cover the gamut of what takes place. As they say, your mileage may vary depending upon which state you live in.

First, you need to achieve a minimum age to seek out getting a driver's license, which is typically around the age of 16 or 17. Why do we do this? The belief is that only someone that has reached the mid-teens is cognitively ready to drive a car. You need to be able to mentally contend with the driving act, along with the roadways and the crazy antics of other drivers, plus be on the watch for pesky pedestrians. There's a lot of cognitive work involved.

You also need to be able to appropriately deal with the physical driving aspects, such as being able to use the brakes, the accelerator pedal, and the steering wheel. This requires not just physical size to reach those driving controls, but also a dexterity and a command of your body agility to do so. Your mind has to be able to tell your arms and hands to steer, and your arm and hands need to respond promptly and accurately.

The age requirement is really a surrogate for whether or not you as a human seem ready to tackle the serious and life-or-death decisions that need to be made when driving a multi-ton car on our roads. Admittedly, I've seen some 16- or 17-years old's that are driving a car and for which I would not have trusted them to do something as simple as rake leaves or chew gum. Thus, it is not just the age per se that decides whether you can drive, and there are other steps involved that hopefully wean out those that aren't ready for the task.

As an aside, my children, now past their teens, interestingly look upon teens in a suspicious manner as drivers. With several years now of driving under their own belts, they have expressed amazement at times that we as a society seem to let many teens drive among us. I'm pretty sure they would support moving up the driving age to at least 18 or even more. Seems that one's perspective changes over time on such matters, I suppose.

In any case, once you've reached the minimum age, you can formally apply to get a driver's license. You don't have to do so, in the sense that if you want to wait until you are older to drive, you can wait until then to apply.

I recall debates with other parents that were insistent they did not want their own children to start driving until at least 17 or possibly waiting until the age of 18. The rationale was that it was safer for their own child and they were trying to do the right thing by deferring them driving until a riper age (the offspring did not necessarily see things this way, as you might imagine).

You need to then show proof of residency in the state that you are applying for a driver's license. This makes sense due to my earlier point about the states being in the driver's seat when it comes to the licensing of human drivers.

States generally will only license those that live in their own state. There are various exceptions related to out-of-state drivers and other complications, but the norm is you need to be a resident in the state for which you are seeking a driver's license.

Often, you need to show proof that you have taken a driver's education (driver ed) course. When I was in high school, the school provided a driver's ed class that the students could take. We even had car simulators that we used in a lab. These were pod-like contraptions that had a steering wheel and the brake and accelerator pedal. There was a film shown on a large screen at the front of the room that portrayed a driver's view of driving on a freeway or street or wherever. You were supposed to drive your fixed-in-place pod as though you were abiding by what was shown on the screen.

Today's teenagers would likely recoil in shock and horror at the primitive nature of these simulators. You could actually steer however you wanted, and it had no impact whatsoever on what the film that was showing at the front of the room. The only way that you could get caught messing around was the instructor had a master panel that displayed the actions of each student in their simulator. If you were ramming on the brakes when you were supposed to be accelerating, the instructor could see via red and green lights on their display board what you were doing, and you'd hear the instructor yell out your name (you didn't want that to happen, I assure you).

One day, we were all properly steering and using our pedals, which after a while became second nature and you went along with it, no whining, no complaining, just do what the instructor expected you to do. I remember this particular day well because of what happened next. The room was usually relatively quite as all the students sat in their pods and concentrated on following along what was being shown on the front screen. Unbeknownst to us, this particular film involved a car that was going to crash into the back of a truck.

Keep in mind that the crashing of the car would simply be that the film at the front of the room would suddenly turn a corner visually and you'd smash into a truck. There was nothing physical about it for those of us in our pod simulators. No tactile feedback of any kind. Well, the instructor decided that maybe we should have some kind of feedback. Just when the film showed us all ramming into the truck, he had arranged for a bunch of metal trash cans to be stacked up at the back of the room, behind us all, and he kicked over those metal clanking cans. I dare say everyone's heart stopped. We thought somehow, we had actually hit that truck!

Some states don't require any driver's ed, some do. Some require it depending upon the age at which you apply. Of those states that do require driver's ed, some allow a wide variety of means to fulfill the requirement, while other states are specific about what the content must be, how many hours long it is, and so on.

Another step that you normally must undertake is agreeing to the rules of the road and acknowledging that you are being granted a privilege to drive in that state. This is something we often don't give much attention toward.

Many people seem to think that you have a right to drive a car, as though there is an amendment to the constitution that says every person has the constitutional right to drive. Kind of funny to think that the founders of our constitution might have envisioned a day in which cars would be roaming our land and they might have snuck something such as: We, the People of the United States, in Order to form a more perfect Union, do declare that all shall have the right to drive a car.

Anyway, the state can revoke your privilege to drive. This is handy as a means of trying to enforce the rules of driving. Abide by the rules, and you are allowed to legally drive. Don't abide by the rules, and you'll lose those driving privileges you were granted. Obviously, it then becomes crucial that drivers know what the rules are, else they can hardly be expected to follow them.

For most of the states, you need to pass several kinds of tests to be able to get your driver's license.

There is usually a vision test. This is to make sure that you can see the road and ably navigate the world in which you are driving. When you ponder the nature of the driving task, it is very visually oriented. We depend almost entirely on what we see. Sure, you are supposed to be listening too, such as hearing the sound of an approaching siren of a police car, but overall it is sight that preoccupies our senses when driving a car.

There is usually a written test that questions your knowledge about driving of a car. Most such written tests involve identifying various street signs and roadway infrastructure situations. There are also questions about the rules or laws in that state about driving, which ties back to the earlier step about agreeing to abide by the rules or laws. In theory, the driver's written test will help ensure that you have studied the rules and laws. To pass the written test, you need to score a certain minimum number right, and it is typically a timed test. If you fail, there are often a limited number of retries allowed right away, and then a waiting period to take the written test again.

These written knowledge tests are often only 20 to maybe 50 questions in size. Can you really test to make sure that a person taking the test knows all of the various street signs (hundreds of those), various traffic or roadway infrastructures (hundreds of those), and the entire body of rules and driving laws (thousands of those), doing so with just a few handfuls of written questions? It does seem suspect.

Admittedly, it is just a random selection of questions and hopefully is sufficient to detect whether someone knows much or not about the whole matter. Regrettably, there are ways to study just for the test, and for which avoids having to know the larger body of elements, but anyway it seems to be sufficient and somehow does the trick.

I know adults that take the test and carp that they had to read the DMV (Department of Motor Vehicles) booklet about our driving regulations, insisting that they've been driving for decades and must ergo know the rules subliminally (therefore not needing to take the test, while the counter-argument is that you should readily pass the test if the rules are so well-ingrained in you).

There is usually a driver's roadway test. This involves getting into your car and having a human passenger that is your tester, grading you as you drive around the local area of the test. I've often wondered whether these testers enjoy this job or live in continual fear of it. You are putting your life into the hands of a complete stranger. In the case of an as yet licensed driver, you already know that the driver is not yet versed in driving and the odds of something going afoul is sizable. Seems like you would need to have nerves of steel.

The driving or roadway test often involves executing stipulated driving actions. You might need to do several right turns, and several left turns. You might need to showcase a U-turn. You are expected to be obeying all the road signs and paying attention to those road signs. You are likely to be asked to drive in a neighborhood and then onto a busy street or highway. The whole thing is nerve wracking for the driver since they are betting their entire dream of getting a license on a few minutes of driving time.

I remember how nervous my own children were. Not because they didn't feel like they could drive well, but simply due to the notion of someone eagle-eye watching your every move and dissecting the littlest wrong movement. The situation does not lend itself to calm driving. There is also the random element of the tester and their personality and perspective. I've seen circumstances of a "cool" tester that purposely tries to put the driver at ease, while there are other "harsh" testers that seem to go out of their way to intimidate and unnerve the driver.

I remember that in my own case I happened to get one of those harsher testers. I know it sounds like sour grapes, but I swear to you it's true that the tester was over-the-top in terms of being deriding. I did pass the driving roadway test, but I lost a point. When I was making a right turn onto a highway, I judged that it was safe to do so, eyeing oncoming traffic and waiting until a good moment presented itself. The tester deducted a point because they felt that though I made a safe choice, in their judgment they would have waited longer. I didn't dispute the matter, since I had passed, though it has stuck in my craw all these years.

Back to the steps about getting certified as a driver, once you've done all of the aforementioned steps, you do a few other paperwork things and ultimately are granted the driver's license. In some states, there is an initial probationary period, during which the tiniest infraction can get your driver's license revoked. In some states, you are able to drive before you take the tests, doing so on a probationary basis, though this usually requires that a licensed driver be in the car with you whenever you are driving.

If it's been a long time since you got your driver's license, I'm guessing that the aforementioned steps bring back either fond memories or memories you'd just as soon forget.

Recall that I've mentioned that there is the car driver certification and there is the car certification. In terms of the car certification, though a car might be certified to be on our roadways, this does not mean that the car is "perfect" in terms of how it works and will perform on the roads. When buying a car or leasing one, most people will often seek out reviews of the brand and model of car, helping them to be aware of the strengths and weaknesses of the car.

You can be a good driver that is driving a "lousy" car. Or, you can be a bad driver that is driving a "good" car. It's a duality.

The duality is important to keep in mind.

Today, as you know, cars don't yet drive themselves (more on this in a moment). Humans drive cars. If a car is unsafe, the driver can be at the whim of what the car can or cannot do. A seasoned race car driver, presumably an expert-level driver, can be undermined by a car that is not performing well. Likewise, a car that is well-tuned and operating at top shape, can be undermined by the acts of a poor driver, one that is either not versed in the driving of that car brand or model, or one that is distracted while driving, or drunk, etc.

Whenever there is a car accident, you cannot immediately leap to a conclusion that it was caused by the driver per se, since it could be that the car itself failed and there was no action feasible by the driver to avoid getting into the accident. You need to consider the car and what its condition was, along with the driver and their condition. Keep this duality in mind as I progress further into this discussion.

What does this have to do with AI self-driving cars?

At the Cybernetic AI Self-Driving Car Institute, we are developing AI software for self-driving cars. One of the most vital and somewhat vexing questions that we face as a society involves the certification of AI self-driving cars.

Allow me to elaborate.

I'd like to first clarify and introduce the notion that there are varying levels of AI self-driving cars. The topmost level is considered Level 5. A Level 5 self-driving car is one that is being driven by the AI and there is no human driver involved. For the design of Level 5 self-driving cars, the auto makers are even removing the gas pedal, brake pedal, and steering wheel, since those are contraptions used by human drivers. The Level 5 self-driving car is not being driven by a human and nor is there an expectation that a human driver will be present in the self-driving car. It's all on the shoulders of the AI to drive the car.

For self-driving cars less than a Level 5, there must be a human driver present in the car. The human driver is currently considered the responsible party for the acts of the car. The AI and the human driver are co-sharing the driving task. In spite of this co-sharing, the human is supposed to remain fully immersed into the driving task and be ready at all times to perform the driving task. I've repeatedly warned about the dangers of this co-sharing arrangement and predicted it will produce many untoward results.

Let's focus herein on the true Level 5 self-driving car. Much of the comments apply to the less than Level 5 self-driving cars too, but the fully autonomous AI self-driving car will receive the most attention in this discussion.

Here's the usual steps involved in the AI driving task:

- Sensor data collection and interpretation
- Sensor fusion
- Virtual world model updating
- AI action planning
- Car controls command issuance

Another key aspect of AI self-driving cars is that they will be driving on our roadways in the midst of human driven cars too. There are some pundits of AI self-driving cars that continually refer to a utopian world in which there are only AI self-driving cars on the public roads. Currently there are about 250+ million conventional cars in the United States alone, and those cars are not going to magically disappear or become true Level 5 AI self-driving cars overnight.

Indeed, the use of human driven cars will last for many years, likely many decades, and the advent of AI self-driving cars will occur while there are still human driven cars on the roads.

This is a crucial point since this means that the AI of self-driving cars needs to be able to contend with not just other AI self-driving cars, but also contend with human driven cars. It is easy to envision a simplistic and rather unrealistic world in which all AI self-driving cars are politely interacting with each other and being civil about roadway interactions.

That's not what is going to be happening for the foreseeable future. AI self-driving cars and human driven cars will need to be able to cope with each other.

Returning to the topic of the certification of AI self-driving cars, let's consider key aspects on this controversial and as yet unsolved problem.

First, take a look at Figure 1.

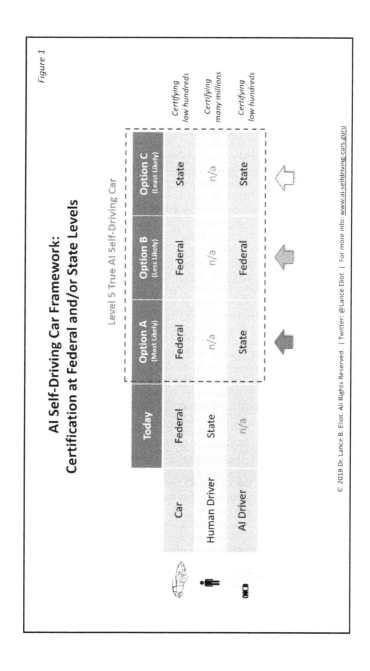

Figure 1

Today, as I already mentioned, the federal government certifies the car, while the state government certifies or licenses the human driver. I've earlier provided various reasons why this makes sense, beyond just the tradition of the matter.

Once we have true AI self-driving cars at a Level 5, who should be certifying or licensing the AI driver?

It's a serious question. I say that it is serious because sometimes people laugh when I ask the question. There laughter stems from the notion that the AI is a kind of robot, though not one you necessarily see in the self-driving car (it's not a walking-talking physical robot), and they find it hard to imagine that you would give a driver's license test to a robot.

Yes, go ahead for a moment and make-up your own stories on this. There you are at the DMV, waiting patiently to take the written test to get your driver's license, and standing in front of you is this six-foot-tall robot, clutching the DMV study booklet, also waiting in line to take the test. The robot looks furtively around.

Glancing at you, the robot whispers to you in a small mechanical sounding voice and asks you what the roadway sign is for a washed-out road. You are torn about whether to give the answer to the robot. Maybe if you help this robot to pass the test, you are helping to put something onto our roadways that you believe shouldn't be driving on our streets. On the other hand, your worried that if you don't answer the question, the muscular robot might pick you up by your neck and toss you outside the DMV. Yikes, those robots!

Returning to reality, let's dispense with the robot imaginary for now.

Assume that an auto maker or tech firm has developed an AI self-driving car. The AI does the driving. There is no human driver for this brand of car. Any humans that get into the AI self-driving car are there strictly as passengers. They can tell the AI where they want to be driven, they can even offer suggestions to the AI about the driving act, yet nonetheless it is the AI that will be driving the self-driving car.

How do you as a human passenger know that the AI can readily, properly, and appropriately drive that AI self-driving car?

And, it's not just the human passengers that care about this. If I am driving a car on the streets of Los Angeles, and there are AI self-driving cars driving on those same streets, how do I know that the AI can readily, properly and appropriately drive those self-driving cars?

Pedestrians on the streets of Los Angeles want to also know that the AI self-driving car coming down the road is being driven by an AI that can readily, properly and appropriately drive that self-driving car.

We have lots of humans that need to be reassured that the AI of the self-driving car "knows" what it is doing, including passengers in that AI self-driving car, and human drivers of other nearby cars, and human pedestrians that are nearby the AI self-driving car, and so on.

If you like, you could even extend this concern to non-humans, such as dogs and cats that might be running out into the street. Will the AI recognize them and drive in an evasive and safe manner as a human driver might?

You can further extend this to non-human's non-animals, such as other AI systems that are driving other AI self-driving cars. Allow me to explain this point.

You've got auto maker X that makes model Q of an AI self-driving car. Another auto maker Z makes their own model R of an AI self-driving car. The AI that is driving Q is not at all the same as the AI that is driving R. Each of the auto makers has taken their own approach to making their own proprietary AI driving systems.

How does the AI of self-driving car model Q "know" that the model R is being driven by an AI that is readily, properly, and appropriately able to drive that self-driving car of auto maker Z?

The answer right now is that it is a wild west and there is not any as yet a defined or agreed upon means of certifying the AI driving skills of a self-driving car.

As a crude form of analogy, suppose someone took their teenager and opted to teach them how to drive a car, and at some point, the parent figured the teenager was ready to drive on our public roadway unimpeded and unaided. If the parent filled-out some paperwork and submitted it to a governing body, let's say it was the state in which they were doing the driving, and the parent attested that the teenager was ready to drive, the state would review the documentation and then decide whether to allow the teenager to now be certified or licensed to drive.

There might not be any testing done by the governing body and they would rely solely on the documentation provided by the parent. Substitute the word "parent" for the auto maker, and substitute "teenager" for the AI driving systems, and that's pretty much the situation we are faced with today as it relates to AI self-driving cars.

Before I unpack that aspect, let's revisit the question of whom is going to be certifying the AI driving systems.

It could be that the states each take on the role of doing the driver certification -- of course, this has been the role that the states undertake for human drivers. Some though wonder whether the states ought to be doing so. Maybe the federal government ought to be doing the AI driving systems certifications. Why, you might ask?

In the case of human drivers, there are millions of those. Furthermore, those millions of human drivers presumably need to be assessed by the state to make sure that those human drivers meet the requirements of the state and are versed sufficient to drive in that state. It's kind of a factory of trying to deal with those millions of human drivers.

In the case of AI driving systems, presumably we'll only have as many as there are AI self-driving car models. Let's guess that it will be in the low hundreds, using the fact that today there are about 250 or so brands of cars in the United States.

The states no longer would seem to need to be geared up to handle millions of drivers (those humans), and instead would only need to focus on hundreds of drivers (AI driving systems). This also assumes a situation whereby AI self-driving cars become prevalent and there are less and less human drivers to be certified.

Perhaps it would be more economical to have the federal government certify or issue a driver's license (or equivalent) for the AI driving systems, rather than the states. You could argue that based on my point earlier about duality, the AI is now wrapped into the car. The feds were already doing the certification of the car, and so the AI aspects are simply a natural extension. It would be likened to adding a new bell-and-whistle to a car and expecting that the feds would be certifying the new feature, rather than the states doing so.

You might counter-argue that the AI is not akin to adding a new kind of windshield wiper or anything of that ilk. The AI is driving the car. It is akin to the act of a human driver. Therefore, the certification of the AI needs to be undertaken by the state. Plus, since it is expected by the state that the AI will drive the car as required by the state regulations, the state has a stake in making sure that the AI is indeed ready for and appropriate to be driving in their state.

There are some that even extend this logic and suggest that perhaps the state ought to certify the car and the car driver (the AI) altogether, since the state is getting dragged into the certification of the AI. In other words, if we aren't going to distinguish the AI from the car, and we consider the AI and the self-driving car to be one integral whole, maybe it is the case that the state should be certifying the entire duality. I mention this notion for completeness, but there are few that take such an extreme view.

It is a conundrum.

While pondering this question about whom is going to be doing the certification, let's also consider an equally juicy and vexing question of how the certification is to be undertaken.

For human drivers, I've already mentioned the nine major steps that they must normally perform to be able to get a driver's license. Of those nine steps, there are some steps that involve testing by the certifying entity, the state, in terms of whether the driver (human) seems ready and able to be a licensed driver.

Humans usually need to pass a vision test. Right now, there is no equivalent to a vision test as administered by a certifying entity for an AI self-driving car. What does a vision test have to do with an AI self-driving car?

You could assert that the equivalent would be a test of the sensory capabilities of an AI self-driving car. An AI self-driving car has cameras and a subsystem devoted to processing visual images. Perhaps that vision processing system should be subject to testing by the entity that might do the certification of the AI driving system. It's a "vision test" of an AI self-driving car's vision capability.

Prudently, you would likely enlarge the notion of the vision test to include the other sensory capabilities of the AI self-driving car. We know that vision is crucial, and it is the primary sense used by humans to drive a car, meanwhile for an AI self-driving car it is likely there will also be radar, ultrasonic, LIDAR, and possibly other sensors too, all of which are crucial to the AI driving system. Each and all of those sensors might be broadly placed into the idea of a "vision test" equivalent for an AI self-driving car.

Human drivers usually need to pass a written knowledge test about their driving awareness and understanding. Should there be an equivalent for AI self-driving cars?

Take a look at Figure 2.

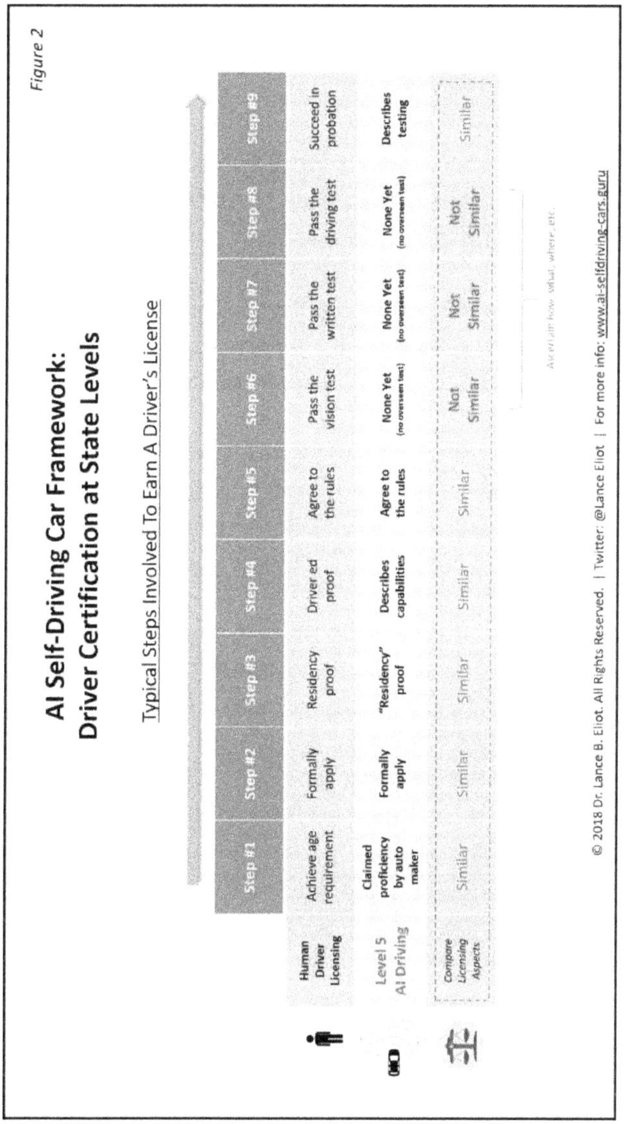

Figure 2

AI Self-Driving Car Framework:
Driver Certification at State Levels

Typical Steps Involved To Earn A Driver's License

	Step #1	Step #2	Step #3	Step #4	Step #5	Step #6	Step #7	Step #8	Step #9
Human Driver Licensing	Achieve age requirement	Formally apply	Residency proof	Driver ed proof	Agree to the rules	Pass the vision test	Pass the written test	Pass the driving test	Succeed in probation
Level 5 AI Driving	Claimed proficiency by auto maker	Formally apply	"Residency" proof	Describes capabilities	Agree to the rules	None Yet (no overseen test)	None Yet (no overseen test)	None Yet (no overseen test)	Describes testing
Compare Licensing Aspects	Similar	Similar	Similar	Similar	Similar	Not Similar	Not Similar	Not Similar	Similar

As in all: how, what, where, etc.

Right now, states are tending towards asking for documentation from the auto maker or tech firm, doing so to gauge what the auto maker or tech firm claims their AI system "knows" about.

This though does not necessarily involve testing of those aspects. Instead, it tends to be more of a paper-based review, rather than any kind of "test" to ensure that the AI system has or does what the documentation claims that it does.

Should there be a "knowledge" test administered by the certifying entity to an AI driving system for which an auto maker or tech firm is trying to get certified to drive on the public roadways?

And, what about the infamous and terrifying roadway driving test that is administered to human drivers seeking a driver's license. Should a certifying entity require that an AI self-driving car be taken on a road test by the certifying entity, similar to what is done with human drivers?

At first glance, I am guessing that you might be tempted to say that sure, the certifying entity ought to conduct the vision test, or more broadly tests of the AI sensory systems of the self-driving car, and ought to have the AI undertake some kind of written knowledge test, and ought to have the AI self-driving car undergo a roadway test. This seems like a prudent action. The more the merrier in terms of trying to make sure that the AI driving system is up-to-snuff.

We expect human drivers to pass the battery of tests, why not also expect the AI to do so.

Part of the muddiness involves what kinds of tests you would devise for these purposes. How extensive would the tests be? Where and how would the tests be conducted? Can you do sufficient testing to believe that the AI self-driving car is ready to be on the roadways?

Recall that I had earlier mentioned that human drivers are administered a written test of maybe 20 to 50 questions, and we agreed that this is a rather small subset of the wide range of knowledge that we expect humans to have about driving. Do we feel the same about having such a short shrift when testing an AI driving system?

For the roadway driving test, the human tester of the DMV perhaps observes the human driver for about 30 minutes or so. Would that be sufficient for assessing the capabilities of an AI driving system?

If you are going to do more extensive testing, the odds are that the state testing would require more elaborated testing development, far beyond the kind of testing done today with human drivers. One argument is that maybe have the federal government could do core testing of the AI driving system, and have the states do an augmented testing that examines the state-specifics. Or, another idea is that the federal certification would encompass the state-specifics and indicate which states the AI self-driving car was certified to drive in.

For human drivers, once you are a licensed driver in any of the states, you pretty much can readily drive in another state, doing so without having to get an additional driver's license.

One concern about AI self-driving cars and testing would be that if a state certified the AI driving system, and suppose that another state does not acknowledge that as a valid certification for AI self-driving cars in their state, it would mean that when your AI self-driving car reached the border of that other state, the AI self-driving car would need to come to a halt and not enter into that state. If the AI self-driving car continued ahead into the other state, doing so would mean that the AI was unlicensed and illegally driving in that state.

Another factor to consider is whether or not we are expecting that the AI of a true AI self-driving car to be able to use common sense reasoning and otherwise have human-like qualities of a sort.

If that's the case, we might need to concoct some kind of Turing Test, which is a long-time and muchly debated means of trying to ascertain whether an AI system is human-like in its cognitive output.

There are additional twists about the testing of AI self-driving cars for certification purposes.

One means of the roadway testing by a human tester would be to do the same as normally is undertaken with human drivers, namely driving on public roadways. This is practical because most DMV's are not perchance next door to a closed track or proving grounds that could be used for the testing. That being said, some DMV's require the driver to first do some parking lot driving, essentially akin to doing a limited closed track test.

So, would the AI driving system be tested on the public roadways or instead (or in addition) be tested on a closed track? If it is a closed track, would this be within the confines of state doing the certification, or could be it be outside of that state (since the state might not have such facilities available). Would the closed track be the only done within the proving grounds testing or would it be done in conjunction with public roadways testing?

Another approach to testing could be the use of simulations. The certifying entity might establish a simulation that encompasses driving in their state, and then have the AI driving system have to take that test. The advantage is that the simulation could force the AI to drive millions upon millions of miles, doing so far beyond what might be feasible in roadway driving tests. An obvious downside is that the simulation is not necessarily the same as actual roadway aspects, though you might combine some amount of simulation with some amount of actual roadway testing.

If the AI self-driving car makes use of remote operators, either for controlling the driving of the self-driving car in emergency circumstances or as an augmentation that provides at times guidance to the AI, would this aspect also be encompassed by the testing? One would assume so.

One concern about any of the testing is that the AI you are testing is not necessarily the same AI that will be driving the self-driving car.

If the AI has Machine Learning or Deep Learning capabilities, it is going to be changing over time, doing so by hopefully improving as it "learns" more and more about driving. We don't know for sure that the AI is going to become better at driving and could actually get worse or introduce nuances that can get itself into trouble.

There are also going to be updates made to the AI system, typically by the use of OTA (Over-The-Air) electronic communications. The OTA is a two-way street. The AI self-driving car can upload data into the cloud such as the collected sensory data. And, the cloud of the auto maker or tech firm can download into the AI self-driving car any patches or updates. This can happen whenever the auto maker or tech firm believes such updates are needed.

Thus, whenever the certifying entity tests the AI driving system, it is only testing at a particular point in time. What about five minutes later? Five days later? Five months later?

Those that aren't worried about this changing AI system aspect are often quick to point out that humans also change, and yet we don't seem overly concerned about right away retesting them. Sure, when their driver's license comes up for renewal every few years, depending upon what their driving records indicates and how long it has been since they were tested, they might be required to do a retest. These such pundits would say that the same can be applied to AI driving systems.

This is not an entirely satisfying argument though, as we aren't as sure, as one would well argue, about how the AI will be changing versus in the aggregate about human drivers changing over time.

Here's another interesting twist. When a certifying entity is trying to test an AI self-driving car, how far can they go in doing so? Can they go beyond the normal everyday driving acts and push the boundaries of what might happen while driving a car? These are at times referred to as edge or corner cases.

For example, suppose the front cameras of the self-driving car are suddenly unable to function, maybe obscured by dirt or perhaps they were hit by flying debris. How well does the AI handle this aspect? Is that a proper test by the certifying entity?

I know that some would argue that there is no equivalent for human drivers during their certification testing, namely the DMV tester doesn't suddenly blind one eye of the human driver or toss mud onto the windshield. Again, I don't buy into this kind of assertion, and instead believe that we can and should hold the AI to a higher standard of testing.

A somewhat brazen aspect being voiced by some pundits involves having a third party or some set of designated third parties that would do the certification testing of AI self-driving cars, rather than having a governmental entity do so.

On that point, you might be aware that Consumer Reports (CR) recently released their first-ever review of automated driving systems, which is not the same as autonomous driving but nonetheless signifies this notion of third-party testing aspects. Consumer Reports used their Auto Test Center track, along with nearby freeways, and put several of the latest models through a series of tests. They selected four such cars, the Cadillac CT6, the Tesla X/S/3, the Infiniti QX50/Nissan Leaf, and the Volvo XC40/XC60.

Consumer Reports ranked the tested cars based on a variety of factors including automated driving capability, performance, ease of use, and how the respective systems monitored and reacted to human drivers that should be engaged in the driving task. Here's the Consumer Reports ranking of the four systems tested, listed from highest to lesser on their scale of assessment:

- Cadillac Super Cruise
- Tesla Autopilot
- Nissan/Infiniti ProPilot
- Volvo Pilot Assist

The overall point being that another approach to the certification topic could involve enlisting private companies, non-profits, consortia, or other third parties to perform the certification. This might be done at the behest of a governmental agency or in conjunction with a governmental agency. There are various efforts underway by numerous entities aiming to see if this approach might be viable.

In terms of the states, California is one of a handful of states that has opted to vigorously pursue the matter of AI self-driving cars. Having adopted California Vehicle Code (CVC) section 38750, taking effect on April 2, 2018, the regulations cover the testing and use of self-driving cars in the state.

There are three major portions of the regulation:

- Auto makers or tech firms can seek a testing permit, requiring the presence of a human driver
- Auto makers or tech firms can seek a driverless testing permit
- Auto makers or tech firms can see the deployment license aka public use permit

Conclusion

We collectively need to ascertain how AI self-driving cars should be certified or licensed to drive on our streets. It's a big deal.

For human drivers, the path to becoming licensed as a driver is well-worn and shown to be relatively reliable and valid.

AI self-driving cars present a novelty that the existing licensing has yet to adapt to. There is an inherent duality of the car and the AI that makes trying to separate out their testing problematic. We need to know that we have good cars and good AI drivers, and it would seem that we should go further than simply having the auto maker or tech firm provide us with their own testing results.

Currently, we all rely upon an entity to certify that drivers in the cars next to us are at least minimally certified to be able to drive a car. When you look over and see that empty driver's seat and realize the car next to you is being driven by AI, you ought to feel some comfort that one way or another there was a bona fide and independent process of trying to test and ensure that the AI driving system is up to the task at-hand. That's a rite of passage needed for AI self-driving cars.

.

CHAPTER 6

OFFSHOOTS AND SPINOFFS
AND
AI SELF-DRIVING CAR

CHAPTER 6

OFFSHOOTS AND SPINOFFS

AND

AI SELF-DRIVING CAR

What did we get by landing on the moon?

Smarmy answers are that we got Tang, the oh-so-delicious artificially flavored orange drink mix, and we brought back to earth about 50 pounds of rocks and dirt in the Apollo 11 mission alone. Just recently it was discovered that over the course of our moon landings, we collected from the moon a rock that was actually originally on earth. Yes, the rock was originally here and based on various hypothetical proposals it was strewn to the moon many eons ago, and we happened to find it now and bring it home. It is considered one of the earth's oldest rocks. Welcome home, wayward earth rock.

Seriously, it is hard to imagine that anyone really would though claim that the only benefits from the moon landing consisted of a drink mix and some rocks. I realize that most reasonable people would agree that going to the moon was an incredible human feat. It demonstrated an ability to seek and achieve what at the time was considered a nearly impossible task. The world was focused on something truly inspirational.

Assuming that you tend to agree with those sentiments and acknowledge the otherwise touted benefits of the moon landing efforts, we can certainly then engage in a dialogue about what else came from the monumental undertaking. Let's do this dialogue under the basis that we already concede the huge overall benefits and then consider what other offshoots or spinoffs might also be attributable to the moon traveling.

You'd be relatively safe to argue that the moon effort spurred advances in electronics and in computing. Hardware advances in miniaturization and in the development of specialized chips and processors can be linked to the moon pursuits. Software advances in new programming languages and in the development of real-time mission-critical systems made great strides. Over the decade that involved preparing for the moon and undertaking a series of shorter trips, a lot happened in the progress of computers and in electronics.

I suppose cynics might claim that those advances might have happened even if there wasn't a race to get to the moon. Certainly, it seems plausible that many of the advances would likely have taken place on their own merits, though whether they would have occurred with the same urgency, the same pace, the same intensity, seems quite dubious. Galvanizing attention on an overall goal that forced along the movement of electronics and computers seems likely to have sparked and pushed forward those offshoots and spinoffs more so than if they were merely acting on everyday economic pursuits.

I don't think we have a time machine that would allow us to somehow replay the era and pretend that there was an alternative of not going for the moon, and then see how things fared.

We have satellites today that are essential to our lives, which you could argue came as an offshoot of the moon effort. Some suggest that microwaves and the everyday microwave oven that we warm-up our day-old burritos can be attributed to the moon research.

The list of moon-effort spurred items is rather lengthy and at times perhaps puzzling, such as freeze-dried food (that makes sense for the space missions), cordless tools (hint, they needed portable drills during the moonwalks), scratch resistant lenses (for the space helmets), invisible braces (transparent ceramic materials used in the spacecraft), and so on.

The overarching theme is that sometimes when you are doing one thing, there can be various offshoots and spinoffs, offering a twofer. Your mainstay is your core attention. Meanwhile, additional benefits might arise. Whether you realize there are potential offshoots is another question. Sometimes, an inventor or innovation maker might not even realize that there is a possibility of spinoffs or offshoots. They are so ingrained in their core effort that they see nothing other than the core itself.

Good for them, unless of course there is a benefit that they are missing out on. If you have a twofer in your hands, it can be a shame to not leverage the second or offspring that comes from the original core. This might not hamper or undermine the original core. Instead, it is simply a lost opportunity. It can be an unrealized opportunity and you need to try and decide whether that opportunity was worthy of getting attention or not.

I'll revisit this twofer notion in a moment.

Let's shift our attention right now to another kind of moonshot, namely the efforts to achieve AI self-driving cars. I've repeatedly stated in my writings and presentations that getting to a true AI self-driving car is very hard. Very, very hard. Tim Cook, the CEO of Apple, has been famously quoted as saying that indeed an AI self-driving car is like a moonshot. The odds of success are ambiguous, and it is not a sure thing by any stretch of the imagination.

At the Cybernetic AI Self-Driving Car Institute, we are developing AI software for self-driving cars. In addition, we are identifying offshoots and spinoffs, doing so along with auto makers and other tech firms in this niche.

Allow me to elaborate.

I'd like to first clarify and introduce the notion that there are varying levels of AI self-driving cars. The topmost level is considered Level 5. A Level 5 self-driving car is one that is being driven by the AI and there is no human driver involved. For the design of Level 5 self-driving cars, the auto makers are even removing the gas pedal, brake pedal, and steering wheel, since those are contraptions used by human drivers. The Level 5 self-driving car is not being driven by a human and nor is there an expectation that a human driver will be present in the self-driving car. It's all on the shoulders of the AI to drive the car.

For self-driving cars less than a Level 5, there must be a human driver present in the car. The human driver is currently considered the responsible party for the acts of the car. The AI and the human driver are co-sharing the driving task. In spite of this co-sharing, the human is supposed to remain fully immersed into the driving task and be ready at all times to perform the driving task. I've repeatedly warned about the dangers of this co-sharing arrangement and predicted it will produce many untoward results.

Let's focus herein on the true Level 5 self-driving car. Much of the comments apply to the less than Level 5 self-driving cars too, but the fully autonomous AI self-driving car will receive the most attention in this discussion.

Here's the usual steps involved in the AI driving task:

- Sensor data collection and interpretation
- Sensor fusion
- Virtual world model updating
- AI action planning
- Car controls command issuance

Another key aspect of AI self-driving cars is that they will be driving on our roadways in the midst of human driven cars too. There are some pundits of AI self-driving cars that continually refer to a utopian world in which there are only AI self-driving cars on the public roads. Currently there are about 250+ million conventional cars in the United States alone, and those cars are not going to magically disappear or become true Level 5 AI self-driving cars overnight.

Indeed, the use of human driven cars will last for many years, likely many decades, and the advent of AI self-driving cars will occur while there are still human driven cars on the roads. This is a crucial point since this means that the AI of self-driving cars needs to be able to contend with not just other AI self-driving cars, but also contend with human driven cars.

It is easy to envision a simplistic and rather unrealistic world in which all AI self-driving cars are politely interacting with each other and being civil about roadway interactions. That's not what is going to be happening for the foreseeable future. AI self-driving cars and human driven cars will need to be able to cope with each other.

Returning to the topic of beneficial offshoots or spinoffs, let's consider how the AI self-driving moonshot-like efforts have a twofer built-in.

There can be hardware related offshoots of AI self-driving car efforts, there can be software related offshoots, and there can be "transformative" offshoots.

The transformative offshoots consist of taking some innovation that originated outside of AI self-driving cars, and for which an AI self-driving maker than utilized the innovation and transformed it into something new or novel, thus there is an offshoot potential ingrained in that transformed variant which can be transplanted back into the non-AI self-driving car realm.

Let's begin with a real-world example of an offshoot, in this case one that happens to be hardware related.

There was some eye-catching "offshoot" news recently in the AI self-driving car industry. In particular, Waymo, the Google/Alphabet autonomous vehicle entity, announced it would aim to sell or license its LIDAR sensor technology to third-parties, albeit only if those third-parties agree to not use the technology for AI self-driving car efforts.

For me, this is a loud bang of a starting gun that has gone off to highlight that the race for an AI self-driving car has also got lots of room for offshoots and spinoffs. I'm not suggesting this is the first time that any contender in the AI self-driving car space has ventured beyond their self-driving car pursuits. I am just emphasizing that having the 500-pound gorilla in the AI self-driving car arena make such an announcement is something worthwhile to notice. The clatter emanating from this will inexorably echo and reverberate, and we'll see more of this soon by many others.

Those of you that are versed in LIDAR are already likely familiar with the path that Waymo opted to go, and I'll take a moment to bring everyone else up-to-speed.

LIDAR is considered by many to be an essential type of sensor, combining together Light and Radar (LIDAR). You wouldn't use LIDAR solely as the only sensor on an AI self-driving car and would instead have it act in a complimentary manner with say camera, conventional radar, ultrasonic sensors, and so on.

Take a look at Figure 1 for an overall indication about offshoots.

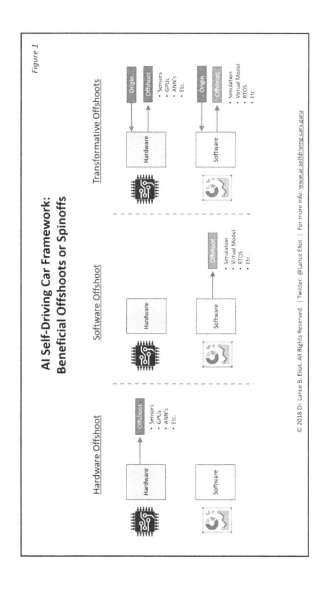

There are many that believe the use of LIDAR is crucial to achieving Level 5, while there are some, most notably Elon Musk and Tesla, asserting otherwise and thus Tesla's aren't outfitted with LIDAR. Musk though has expressed acknowledgment that he might be off-base about LIDAR and we'll all have to wait and see whether his instincts were on-par or not.

In the case of Waymo, they are stanch believers in LIDAR. The use of LIDAR is essential to their AI self-driving aims. As such, they've been pursuing LIDAR since the early days of their initial formation and forays. At the time, they gradually decided that using off-the-shelf LIDARs from vendors was not their preference and so they opted to make their own LIDARs.

Some pundits have congratulated Waymo for taking their own path on LIDAR, allowing Waymo to presumably control and determine what the LIDAR does and how they will make use of it. Given that LIDAR is going to be key to their AI self-driving cars, and if someday they are able to succeed with a true Level 5, and if this translates into potentially millions upon millions of outfitted self-driving cars, their owning the LIDAR puts them into the driver's seat, if you know what I mean.

This is an ongoing debate within many of the AI self-driving car making firms. The debate is as follows.

If you use a sensor like LIDAR and you become dependent upon a vendor to provide it to you, you might be doing so right now to get those prototype AI self-driving cars underway, but what happens if your AI self-driving car efforts really take off into the stratosphere. Suppose everyone wants your AI self-driving car and you are able to grab market share of many millions of such cars. Meanwhile, the maker of the LIDAR is along for the ride.

You could say that the tide rises all boats, meaning that if your AI self-driving car succeeds then the LIDAR maker is looking at a big payday as well. That seems healthy for all parties.

The downside could be that the LIDAR maker becomes the tail wagging the dog. Suppose the LIDAR maker opts to go in some other direction that the AI self-driving car maker isn't keen on, or otherwise there are disputes. The AI self-driving car maker is likely to have so enmeshed the LIDAR particulars into their code that trying to somehow unplug it and plug in some other LIDAR system is not going to be easy. In fact, it could be costly and painful, creating great disruption just as your AI self-driving car is perhaps on the verge of greatness.

On the other hand, some pundits say you'd be crazy as an AI self-driving car maker to devote your attention and precious resources to reinventing the wheel by making your own LIDAR. The number of LIDAR makers is rapidly increasing, and it seems that for each new dawn there is another LIDAR startup someplace. It's hot.

Furthermore, the underlying technology of LIDAR is advancing at an astounding pace. Trying to keep up is daunting. Again, if your mainstay is the AI self-driving car aspects overall, focusing your attention on one particular aspect, the LIDAR, would seem to some as a distraction and worse. It could be worse in that you might not be keeping the same pace as other LIDAR makers and so end-up with something less-than the best that the market can provide.

Those same pundits would argue that if the AI self-driving car is making their own LIDAR, they are likely going to find themselves somewhat trapped in their own petard. Are they going to be able to advance their LIDAR at the same pace as the marketplace? Will they "compromise" to something less-so, wanting to stick with their own efforts. Might they get eclipsed, and yet be mired already in having done their own thing.

It can be a conundrum.

Part of this involves historical momentum too.

In the case of Waymo, they ventured into their own LIDAR at a time when arguably the number of LIDAR options was few. You could try to make the case that they by necessity chose to take the bull by the horn. Whether they would need to do so today, well, that's a different question. And, once they started down the trajectory of their own LIDAR, one might argue that they had sown a path that would be hard to not continue with. It's the same as if getting into bed with a particular LIDAR maker and then that's what you have, though in this case it is of your own invention.

For Waymo, they've made their stand and it consists of having their own customized LIDAR. One of those models is known as the Laser Bear Honeycomb. It is considered a perimeter LIDAR sensor, typically used to sense around the bumper of a self-driving car. This is just one kind of LIDAR sensor and not the whole kit and caboodle that Waymo has in their tech arsenal.

The Laser Bear Honeycomb is considered a 3D LIDAR and has a Field of View (FOV) of 95 degrees on the vertical and 360 degrees on the horizontal. It also uses the multi-return per pulse capabilities that more robust LIDAR units now have, meaning that there is a chance of detecting objects in a more detailed fashion than otherwise by the more simplistic singular returns. The unit also allows for a range of zero (near to) which allows detecting objects immediately in front of the sensor versus some LIDARs that have a minimum distance before returns are able to be detected. If you'd like to see more details about the Laser Bear Honeycomb, take a look at Simon Verghese's posts at the Waymo web site (he's the head of the Waymo LIDAR Team).

I'm not going to delve into how their LIDAR compares to other marketplace options. That's not the focus or theme herein.

The reason I've brought up the Waymo LIDAR and the announcement is due to the offshoot or spinoff notion. You might have noticed that I mentioned earlier that Waymo is restricting who can potentially purchase or license the LIDAR from them. They are excluding uses of the LIDAR for AI self-driving cars.

Why, you might be wondering? Simply stated, they aren't willing to handover their own "secret sauce" to other AI self-driving car makers. If they did, one could argue that they would be essentially undermining their own efforts by arming competitors with the same armaments that they themselves possess. It might be likened to handing your special ICBM to someone else that can then use it to get to your level and possibly even surpass you.

One could also argue that they are perhaps better off not having other AI self-driving car makers use their LIDAR since they might get bogged down into dealing with those other AI self-driving car makers. In essence, suppose that they sold the LIDAR to the AI self-driving car maker X, and X began to toy with it and wanted to ascertain more deeply how it works and what it can do. In the act of doing so, would Waymo inadvertently spill the beans on other salient aspects of their own AI self-driving car efforts? It would be a possibility, and a dangerous and undesirable slippery slope.

Okay, so we have a major AI self-driving car making entity that is willing to provide as an offshoot or spinoff their own proprietary LIDAR, as long as it is used for anything but AI self-driving cars (there might be other restrictions they'll eventually land on, which depends on what third parties approach them about the possible usage). Right now, Waymo is indicating that they anticipate the LIDAR could be used in diverse ways such as for robotics, in the area of physical security, in the use of agriculture applications, and so on.

Those seem plausible and it will be interesting to watch and see what takes hold.

As an aside, I was asked about the announcement while I was speaking at an industry conference and the question was about the money side of this matter.

Specifically, the question was whether Waymo needed the money or revenue to keep in business and therefore they were now "desperately" seeking to leverage their technology. I held back my laughter. It is hard to imagine Waymo might do this because they are running low on cash and figured by selling LIDARs they could keep the lights on and still provide those green tea Frappuccino's to the staff.

As mentioned earlier, sometimes a firm will have a twofer and realize the secondary or offshoot value that the core innovation has. The realization of a twofer means that you can put your toe into the water and see what happens. If the secondary or offshoot potential begins to seem viable and the marketplace laps it up, great. If the marketplace doesn't seem to be able to find a use for it, well, you now know, and meanwhile you've been continuing to use it for your own core efforts.

You could even claim that it is a bit of rolling the dice without taking too much risk. Suppose that someone else discovers a fantastic way to use your tech. It becomes a huge smashing success in some other endeavor, one that you might not have ever considered on your own. Indeed, it could become its own tail wagging the dog, meaning that it somehow surpasses your own use of it and the true mission of the innovation is leveraged in a completely different way.

That doesn't happen very often. But it's a roll of the dice and likely worth seeing how the roll comes out.

There's another angle on this too. It could be that while floating out the innovation to the marketplace, you end-up getting feedback that otherwise you would have been unlikely to get on your own. Regardless of how good your own internal team might be, there are chances that others mulling over your innovation, those newcomers external to your own resources, might come up with fresh ideas that could further burnish its value.

One could argue the counter-punch that suppose the marketplace finds flaws or blemishes that you had not identified, or that you identified and perhaps downplayed internally. Wouldn't that undermine your innovation? I'd say no. If an innovation is still early in its life cycle, you likely would want to know about any such issues, hopefully surfacing those issues and correcting them before you get too much further along. The later that you discover such guffaws, the worse it usually will be, in terms of cost, time, and other factors.

I'm shifting away now herein about the Waymo announcement and want to cover other facets overall about offshoots and spinoffs, along with identifying other kinds of such aspects that might occur in the AI self-driving car arena.

Per my overall framework mentioned earlier, there could be offshoots in any of the realms of an AI self-driving car, encompassing the sensors, the sensor fusion, the virtual world model updating, the AI action planning, the car controls commands issuance, and too in the areas of the strategic AI, the self-aware AI, etc.

The sensors aspects are the ripest for an offshoot. If you are making a sensor that you devised specifically for AI self-driving cars, the odds are high that such a sensor can be used in other ways and other means. The most obvious would be in other kinds of Autonomous Vehicles (AV), such as using your sensor in an autonomous drone or an autonomous submersible vehicle.

Using your sensor in another family-related AV's is not much of a stretch, admittedly. Presumably, those should be ways that already jump out at you.

A more pronounced stretch would be to consider using your sensors in something other than a vehicle. Move your mindset away from vehicles and consider how else might the sensor be used. Could it be an Internet of Things (IoT) device that might be used in the workplace? Or maybe in the home? There is no doubt that the IoT marketplace is enormous and growing, so perhaps you can re-apply your sensor into that space.

One of the difficulties often times about brainstorming about other uses of your own internally developed innovation is that you might fall into a groupthink trap. If everyone on your team was brought to the table to develop a sensor for purposes of Y, they are likely steeped in the matter of Y. It's all they think about it. It's what they know best.

Trying to get them to go outside the box of Y is not usually readily done. In fact, sometimes they can be forceful about staying inside the box. This makes sense since they know the specific requirements that they built the thing for. When you try to suggest it might be used for Z or Q instead, it can generate acrimonious replies about the ten or twenty reasons why it cannot be used for those other purposes.

They might be right, they might be wrong.

You need to ferret out whether in fact trying to use the innovation for other purposes might be inappropriate, or whether it is just a hesitation based on an anchoring to what the team already knows. This can be difficult to discern. Trying to shoehorn an innovation into other uses might not be productive, and worse still might be untoward.

I've worked with some top tech leaders that were constantly coming up with new (and often wild) ideas about how they could repurpose their innovation. They'd be eating a meal and come up with another idea. They'd be on the phone and suddenly come up with an idea. They were like miniature idea generating factories.

At times this was handy and provided opportunity for adapting the innovation to some other notable use. In other cases, it was as though the innovation was a swiss army knife that could be used in a thousand ways, when the reality was that it was simply a toothpick and did not have any of the other tools, lacking a can opener, a knife, a screwdriver, and so on. I'm not saying that they could not have ultimately adapted the innovation, only that the distance was greater than was in the mind of the top leaders.

Sometimes bringing an innovation to the marketplace can be a fresh dose of reality to a top leader. Within the firm, perhaps it is hard for the staff to pushback on wild ideas. They don't want to be pigeonholed as a naysayer. By allowing the innovation to touch into the market, it will be the marketplace that provides the needed feedback. This can get top leaders to listen and pay attention when they otherwise might have been hesitant to do so.

The other side of that coin is that sometimes the internal AI developers are so burned out that they cannot imagine taking on something new with their innovation. If you are pouring your heart and soul into a sensor for an AI self-driving car, and you are exhausted in doing so, even if there is a glimmer of promise for the sensor in some other ways, you cannot cope with the added effort that will undoubtedly fall onto your shoulders. Thus, you might subliminally nix the new use, somewhat due to basic survival instincts.

Besides sensors, there is a slew of other hardware that has the potential for being used beyond the realm of AI self-driving cars. There are specialized processors, GPU's, FGPA's, and the like, all of which can be applied to other fields of endeavor.

I realize that many of those hardware advances were already being done for other fields, and then were re-applied into the AI self-driving car niche. I'm not suggesting they were made necessarily initially for AI self-driving cars. In some cases, something that was made for another purpose has been brought into the realm of AI self-driving cars. Once it has been so transformed, it can potentially take on a new life in terms of not only satisfying the needs of AI self-driving cars, but turnaround and use that augmented hardware for other outside aspects that now are opened, which perhaps weren't yet open, prior to the augmentation for the AI self-driving car needs.

My description about the hardware aspects can be readily applicable to the software aspects.

If you develop a simulation for AI self-driving cars, based on crafting a new way of doing simulations, it could be that you can re-apply that capability to other areas. Perhaps the simulation of an AI self-driving car driving in a traffic situation can be readily re-applied to simulating the efforts of a warehouse and the movement of goods within the warehouse. Again, there are some simulation packages that already had that purpose for warehousing, and they were re-applied into AI self-driving cars, but there are some simulations that were built solely focused on AI self-driving cars that I would say could be re-adapted for other uses.

Think about the entire software stack associated with AI self-driving cars. If you are an AI self-driving car maker, and if you have developed various tools and capabilities within that stack, you might be sitting on a potential goldmine of something that you could provide to the marketplace.

You'd need to decide whether or not you want other competing AI self-driving car makers to be able to use your new-to-the-market software. Is it something that provides you with a competitive edge? Would it reveal too much about your secret sauce?

We've of course seen some of the AI self-driving makers that have opted to not only bring an offshoot into the marketplace but even make it available as open source.

For example, at the Autonomous Vehicle (AV) 2019 conference, I had a chance to chat with Hugh Reynolds, Head of Simulation for the Advanced Technologies Group (ATG) of Uber. After having used a number of simulation packages, they developed an internal capability that they decided recently to share with the industry.

He and his team have released as open source version of their Autonomous Visualization System (AVS).

It consists of an element known as XVIZ, which is a spec that deals with the managing of generated AI self-driving car data, and includes their streetscape.gl, which provides a means to build web apps that leverage the data that's based on the XVIZ formats. You can find these tools on GitHub (https://uber.github.io/).

There are already other AI self-driving car makers that have indicated they'll likely be making use of the capability. Since it is open source, this reduces the qualms by those other AI self-driving car makers about necessarily getting locked into something that another maker might otherwise control. Making it open source might seem odd to some, but there is not just some kind of altruism in doing so, the odds are that this will ultimately also help Uber by spurring an ecosystem around the simulation and benefit the simulation by boosting it in ways that Uber itself might not have the time or have considered doing.

In the combination of both software and hardware, we've seen that the Machine Learning and Deep Learning aspects are also spurring offshoots. For AI self-driving cars, one of the most significant elements is the use of deep artificial neural networks, especially in the analysis and interpretation of sensor data. There are software tools and hardware capabilities of Machine Learning and Deep Learning that have been forged within the AI self-driving car space that are gradually coming onto the market for use in other domains.

Suppose that while the engineers and scientists were working on developing the needed innovations and high-tech to get to the moon that they opted to right away do offshoots or spinoffs?

I ask the question because it brings up an important consideration about offshoots and spinoffs. What is the right timing for having an offshoot or spinoff?

Imagine the high-tech moonshot workers in the 1960s that rather than focusing on how to control the space capsule to land on the moon, instead they became attentive to making microwave ovens that could be used in the home. Maybe we would not have gotten to the moon. Or, maybe we would have taken ten more years to get there.

The point being that if you begin to take on the aspect of doing an offshoot or spinoff, there is a chance you are risking keeping to your knitting. You are maybe taking on more than you can chew. The problem could become one of the core getting second fiddle to the offshoot, which might not have been your plan, yet you fell into it, slowly, inexorably, like quicksand.

It is easy to do. Sometimes the offshoot gets all the glory. The core use is already well-accepted within the firm. Most take it for granted. The excitement about seeing your hardware or software applied to a new domain is rather intoxicating. Top leaders can readily get caught up in the allure and begin to inadvertently drain resources and attention away from the core use.

Advances for the core use begin to get pushed aside or delayed. Maybe the quality of the updates or revisions start to lessen. The other use of the core saps the energy and willpower that got the core to where it is. Sure, the other use might be promising, meanwhile sacrifices to the core can undermine the core overall.

I caution top leaders to make sure they have their ducks aligned when they make the decision to forge some kind of offshoot or spinoff. Are they ready to do so? How much of their existing resources will get pulled away to it? Will they provide as much attention to the core as they are to the offshoot, or will they subconsciously starve the core? These are all important matters to be discussed.

The timing question is a tough one to balance. You want to bring out the offshoot while the core is still considered new and worthy. If you wait too long and the core is now already eclipsed by other substitutes in the market, you missed your window of opportunity.

The timing needs to be the vaunted Goldilocks mode, not too early, not too late, just the right temperature, as they say.

Another consideration is whether the innovation if created by an internally focused team is ready to deal with becoming a business within a business. When selling or licensing your innovation to other firms, you suddenly have a whole new enchilada to deal with, meaning that you need to provide service to that customer or set of customers. Is your internal team prepared to deal with external entities that want support or otherwise require a services aspect that your team was not having to do before?

Conclusion

There are some doom-and-gloom pundits that say we will never achieve true AI self-driving cars. We are all on a fool's errand, they contend. Though I disagree with their assessment, I like to point out to them that even if they are right, which I doubt, but even if they are right, the push toward AI self-driving cars is creating numerous benefits that otherwise I assert would not likely exist.

In essence, I am claiming that the race toward true AI self-driving cars has other benefits beyond whether we actually are able to achieve true AI self-driving cars.

One obvious benefit is that conventional cars are getting more automation. As much as that seems good, I've also cautioned that we need to be leery of automating non-self-driving cars to the degree that humans get lulled or fooled into believing the AI can do more than it really can.

AI self-driving cars are an exciting notion that has energized the field of AI.

It has helped move AI out of the backrooms of university labs and into the sunshine.

As a former university professor, I still maintain my roots at numerous universities, and I've seen first-hand how AI self-driving cars are "driving" faculty and students into areas of AI that I believe would not have gotten as much attention otherwise.

Society as a whole has been energized into discussing topics about transportation that I believe would not have been as active or headline catching, were it not for the AI self-driving car efforts. Regulators are considering the advent of AI self-driving cars, which also brings up the topic of mobility and how can our society do more for increasing mobility.

In short, similar to the real moonshot, I'd argue that the advent of AI self-driving cars has become a motivator.

It has inspired attention to not just AI self-driving cars, but encompasses far more, including societal, business, economic, and regulatory aspects.

This inspiration sparks innovators, dreamers, engineers, scientists, economists, and all of the myriad of stakeholders that AI self-driving cars touch upon.

Whether you will grant me that the race toward AI self-driving cars has produced those aspects or not, at least perhaps we can agree that the advances made in AI, along with hardware and software, are having and will likely continue to have a profound spillover effect.

The number of offshoots and spinoffs will gradually increase, and I predict you'll see that the AI self-driving car pursuit produces more than you might have anticipated.

I don't think we'll look back and say that all we got was Tang, and instead we'll be saying that without the AI self-driving car pursuit we wouldn't have amazing advances that we'll be relishing in the future. Admittedly, there won't be moon rocks to look at, but it will still be good, mark my words.

CHAPTER 7

DEPERSONALIZATION

AND

AI SELF-DRIVING CARS

CHAPTER 7

DEPERSONALIZATION

AND

AI SELF-DRIVING CARS

Is automation and in particular AI leading us toward a service society that depersonalizes us?

Some pundits say yes, arguing that the human touch of providing services is becoming scarcer and scarcer, and eventually we'll all be getting served by AI systems that treat us humans as though we are non-human. More and more we'll see and experience that humans will lose their jobs to AI and be replaced by automation that is less costly, and notably less caring, eschewing us as individuals and abandoning personalized service. Those uncaring and heartless AI systems will simply stamp out whatever service is being sought by a human and there won't be any soul in it, there won't be any spark of humanity, it will be push-button automata only.

In my view, those pundits are seeing the glass as only half empty. They seem to not either notice or want to observe that the glass is also half full. Let me share with you some examples of what I mean.

Before I do so, please be aware that the word "depersonalization" can have a multitude of meanings. In the clinical or psychology field, it has a meaning of feeling detached or disconnected from your body and would be considered a type of mental disorder. I'm not using the word in that manner herein. Instead, the theme I'm invoking involves the humanization or dehumanization around us, floating the idea of being personalized to human needs or being depersonalized to them. That's a societal frame rather than a purely psychological portrayal.

With that said, let's use an example to get at my depersonalization and personalization theme.

Banking is an area ripe with prior exhortations of how bad things would become once ATM's took over as there would no longer be in-branch banking with human tellers (that's what was predicted). We would all be slaves to ATM machines. You were going to stand in front of the ATM and yell out "where have all the humans gone?" as you fought with the banking system to perform a desired transaction.

Recently, I went to my local bank branch to make a deposit. I was in a hurry and opted to squeeze in this errand on my way to a business meeting. The deposit was somewhat sizable so I opted to go and perform the transaction with the human teller, rather than feed my deposit into the "impersonal" ATM.

Upon my coming up to the teller window, the teller provided a big smile and welcomed me to the bank. How's my day going, the teller asked. The teller proceeded to mention that it had been a busy morning at the branch. Looking outside the branch window, the teller remarked that it looked like rain was on its way. I wanted to make the deposit and get going, yet could see that the chitchat, though friendly and warm, would keep dribbling along and wasn't seemingly in pursuit of my desired transaction.

I presented my check to be deposited and was asked to first run my banking card through the pad at the teller window. I did so. The teller looked at my info on their screen and noted that I had not talked with one of their bankers for quite a while, offering to bring over a bank manager to say hello. I declined the gracious offer. The teller then noted that one of my CD's was coming due in a month and suggested that I might want to consider various renewal options. Not just now, I demurred.

The teller finally proceeded with the deposit and then, just as I was stepping away to head-out, called me back to mention that they were having a special this week on opening new accounts. Would I be interested in doing so? As you can imagine, in my haste to get going, I quickly said no thanks and tried to make my way to the door. Turns out that the teller had already signaled to the bank manager and I was met at the door with a thanks for coming in by the pleasant manager, along with handing me a business card in case I had any follow-up needs.

Let's unpack or dissect my in-branch experience.

On the one hand, you could say that I was favorably drenched in high-touch service. The teller engaged me in dialogue and tried to create a human-to-human connection. Rather than solely focusing on my transaction, I was offered a bevy of other options and possibilities. My banking history at the bank was used to identify opportunities for me to enhance my banking efforts at the bank. All in all, this would seem to be the picture-perfect example of human personalized service.

Having done lots of systems work in the banking industry, I know how hard it can be to get a branch to provide personalized and friendly service. One bank that I helped fix had a lousy reputation when I first was brought in, known for having branches that were terribly run. Whenever you went into a branch it was like going to a gulag. There were long lines, the tellers were ogres, and you felt as though you were a mere cog in a gigantic wheel of their banking procedures, often making the simplistic banking acts into a torturous affair.

Thus, my recent experience of making my deposit at my local branch should be a shining example of what a properly run bank branch is all about.

If I were to have to choose between the somewhat over-friendly experience versus going to a branch that was like descending into Dante's inferno, I certainly would choose the overly friendly case.

Nonetheless, I'd like to explore more deeply the enriched banking experience. I was in a hurry. The friendly dialogue and attempts to upsell me were getting in the way of a quick in-and-out banking transaction. In theory, the teller should have judged that I was in a hurry (I assure you that I offered numerous overt signals as such) and toned down the ultra-service effort. It is hard perhaps to fault the teller and one might point at whatever pressures there are on the teller to do the banking jingle, perhaps drummed into the teller as part of the training efforts at the bank and likely baked into performance metrics and bonuses.

In any case, I walked out of the branch grumbling and vowed that in the future I would use the ATM. Unfair, you say? Maybe. Am I being a whiner by "complaining" about too much personalized service? Maybe. But it shouldn't be that I have to make a choice between the rampant personalized service versus the utterly depersonalized gulag service. I should be able to choose which suits my service needs at the time of consuming the service.

About a week later, I had to make another deposit and this time used the drive-thru ATM. After entering my PIN, the screen popped-up asking if I was there to make a deposit, and if so, there was a one-click offered to immediately shift into deposit taking mode. I used the one-click, slipped my check into the ATM, it then scanned and asked me to confirm the amount, which I did, and the ATM then indicated that I usually don't get a printed receipt and unless I wanted one this time, it wasn't going to print one out.

I was satisfied that the deposit seemed to have been made and so I put my car into gear and drove on. The entire transaction time must have been around 30 seconds at most, making it many times faster than when I had made a deposit via the teller. I did not have to endure any chitchat about the weather. I was not bombarded with efforts to upsell me. In-and-out, the effort was completed, readily, without fanfare.

Notice that the ATM had predicted that I was there to make a deposit. That was handy. Based on my last several transactions with the bank, the banking system had analyzed my pattern and logically deduced that I was most likely there to make a deposit. And, I was offered a one-click option to proceed with making my deposit, which showcased that not only was my behavior anticipated, the ATM tailored its actions to enable my transaction to proceed smoothly.

Would you say that my ATM experience was one of a personalized nature or a depersonalized nature?

We always tend to assume that whenever something is "depersonalized" that it must be bad. The word has a connotation that suggests something untoward. Nobody wants to be depersonalized. In the case of the ATM, I wasn't asked about the weather and there wasn't a smiling human that spoke with me. I interacted solely with the automation. If that's the case, ergo I must be getting "depersonalized" service, one would assume.

Yet, my ATM experience was actually personalized. The system had anticipated that I wanted to make a deposit. This had been followed-up by making the act of depositing easy. Once I had made the deposit, the ATM did not just spit out a receipt, which often is what happens (and I frequently see deposit receipts laying on the ground near the ATM, presumably leftover by hurried humans). The ATM knew via my prior history that I tended to not get a receipt and therefore the default was going to be that it would not produce one in this instance.

Given the other kinds of more sophisticated patterns in my banking behavior that could be found by using AI capabilities, I thought that this ATM experience was illustrative of how even simple automation can provide a personalized service experience. Imagine what more could be done if we added some hefty Machine Learning or Deep Learning into this.

I've used the case of the banking effort to help illuminate the notion of what constitutes personalization versus depersonalization. Many seem to assume that if you remove the human service provider, you are axiomatically creating a depersonalized service. I don't agree.

The performance of a service act consists of the service provider and the receiver of the service, the customer. Generally, when considering depersonalized service, we think about the service provider as being perfunctory, dry, lacking in emotion, unfeeling, aloof, and otherwise without an expression of caring for the customer. We also then think about the receiver of the service, the customer, and their reaction of presumably becoming upset at the lack of empathy to their plight as they are trying to obtain or consume the service.

I argue that the service provider can provide a personalized or depersonalized service, either one, even if it is a human providing the service. The mere act of having a human provide a service does not make it personalized. I'm sure you've encountered humans that treated you as though you were inconsequential, as though you were on an assembly line, and they had very little if any personalization, likely bordering on or perhaps fully enmeshed into depersonalization.

A month ago, I ventured to use the Department of Motor Vehicles (DMV) office and was amazed at how depersonalized they were able to make things. Each of the human workers in the DMV office had that look as though they would prefer to be anyplace but working in the DMV. The people flowing into the DMV were admittedly rancorous and often difficult to contend with. I'm sure these DMV workers had their fill each day of people that were grotesquely impolite and cantankerous.

In any case, there were signs telling you to stand here, move there, wait for this, wait for that. Similar to getting through an airport screening, this was a giant mechanism to move the masses through the process. I'm sure it was as numbing for the DMV workers as it was for those of us there to get a driver's license transaction undertaken.

See Figure 1 for an overview about the depersonalization topic.

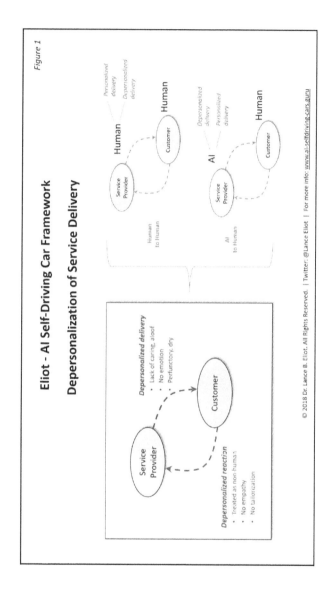

Figure 1

Eliot - AI Self-Driving Car Framework

Depersonalization of Service Delivery

Let's all agree then that you can have a human that provides a personalized or a depersonalized service, which will be contingent on a variety of factors, such as the processes involved, the incentives for the human service provider, and the like.

I'd to like next assert that automation can also provide either a personalized service or a depersonalized service. Those are both viable possibilities.

It all depends upon how the automation has been established. In my view, if you add AI to providing a service, and do it well, you are going to have a solid chance of making that service personalized. This won't happen by chance alone. In fact, by chance alone, you are probably going to have AI service that seems depersonalized.

We might at first assume that the automation is going to be providing a depersonalized service, likewise we might at first assume that a human will provide a personalized service. That's our usual bias. Either of those assumptions can be upended.

Furthermore, it can be tricky to ascertain what personalized versus depersonalized service consists of. In my example about the bank branch and the teller, everything about the setup would seem to suggest a high-touch personalized service. I'm sure the bank spent a lot of money to try and arrive at the high-touch level of service. Yet, in my case, in the instance of wanting to hurriedly do a transaction, the high-touch personalized service actually defeated itself.

That's a problem with having personalized service that is ironically inflexible. It is ironic in that the assumption is that personalized means that you will be incessantly presented with seeming personalization. Instead, the personalization should be based on the human receiving the service and what makes most sense for them. Had the teller picked-up on the aspect that I was in a hurry, it would have been relatively easy to switch into a mode of aiding my transaction and getting me out of the bank, doing so without undermining the overarching notion of personalization.

For those of you that are AI developers, I hope that you keep in mind these facets about depersonalization and personalization. Namely, via AI, you have a chance at making a service providing system more responsive and able to provide personalization, yet if you don't seek that possibility, the odds are that your AI system will appear to be the furtherance of depersonalization.

Humans interacting with your AI system are more likely to be predisposed to the belief that your AI will be depersonalizing.

In that sense, you have a larger hurdle to jump over. In the case of a human providing a service, by-and-large we all tend to assume that it is likely to be imbued with personalization, though for circumstances like the DMV and airport screening we've all gotten used to the idea that you are unlikely to get personalized service in those situations (when it happens, we are often surprised and make special note of it).

You also need to take into account that there is personalization of an inflexible nature, which can then undermine the personalization being delivered. As indicated via the bank branch example, using that as an analogy, consider that if you do have AI that seems to provide personalization, don't go overboard and force whatever monolithic personalization that you came up with onto all cases of providing the service. Truly, personalized service should be personalized to the needs of the customer in-hand.

What does this have to do with AI self-driving cars?

At the Cybernetic AI Self-Driving Car Institute, we are developing AI software for self-driving cars. There are numerous ways in which the AI can either come across as personalized or depersonalized, and it is important for auto makers and tech firms to realize this and devise their AI systems accordingly.

Allow me to elaborate.

I'd like to first clarify and introduce the notion that there are varying levels of AI self-driving cars. The topmost level is considered Level 5. A Level 5 self-driving car is one that is being driven by the AI and there is no human driver involved. For the design of Level 5 self-driving cars, the auto makers are even removing the gas pedal, brake pedal, and steering wheel, since those are contraptions used by human drivers. The Level 5 self-driving car is not being driven by a human and nor is there an expectation that a human driver will be present in the self-driving car. It's all on the shoulders of the AI to drive the car.

For self-driving cars less than a Level 5, there must be a human driver present in the car. The human driver is currently considered the responsible party for the acts of the car. The AI and the human driver are co-sharing the driving task. In spite of this co-sharing, the human is supposed to remain fully immersed into the driving task and be ready at all times to perform the driving task. I've repeatedly warned about the dangers of this co-sharing arrangement and predicted it will produce many untoward results.

Let's focus herein on the true Level 5 self-driving car. Much of the comments apply to the less than Level 5 self-driving cars too, but the fully autonomous AI self-driving car will receive the most attention in this discussion.

Here's the usual steps involved in the AI driving task:
- Sensor data collection and interpretation
- Sensor fusion
- Virtual world model updating
- AI action planning
- Car controls command issuance

Another key aspect of AI self-driving cars is that they will be driving on our roadways in the midst of human driven cars too. There are some pundits of AI self-driving cars that continually refer to a utopian world in which there are only AI self-driving cars on the public roads. Currently there are about 250+ million conventional cars in the United States alone, and those cars are not going to magically disappear or become true Level 5 AI self-driving cars overnight.

Indeed, the use of human driven cars will last for many years, likely many decades, and the advent of AI self-driving cars will occur while there are still human driven cars on the roads.

This is a crucial point since this means that the AI of self-driving cars needs to be able to contend with not just other AI self-driving cars, but also contend with human driven cars. It is easy to envision a simplistic and rather unrealistic world in which all AI self-driving cars are politely interacting with each other and being civil about roadway interactions. That's not what is going to be happening for the foreseeable future. AI self-driving cars and human driven cars will need to be able to cope with each other.

Returning to the topic of depersonalization and personalization, let's consider how AI self-driving cars can get involved in and perhaps mired into these facets.

I was speaking at a recent conference on AI self-driving cars and during the Q&A there was an interesting question or point made by an audience member. The audience member stood-up and derided human drivers that often cut-off bike riders.

She indicated that to get to the conference, she had ridden her bike, which she also rides when going to work (this event was in the Silicon Valley, where bike riding for getting to work is relatively popular). While riding to the convention, she had narrowly gotten hit at an intersection when a car took a right turn and seemed to have little regard for her presence as she rode in the bike lane.

You might assume that the car driver was not aware that she had been in the bike lane and therefore mistakenly cut her off. If that was the case, her point could be that an AI self-driving car would presumably not make that same kind of human error. The AI sensors would hopefully detect a bike rider and then appropriately the AI action planner would attempt to avoid cutting off the bike rider.

It seemed though that she believed the human driver did see her. The act of cutting her off was actually deliberate. The driver was apparently of a mind that the car had higher priority over the bike rider, and thus the car could dictate what was going to happen, namely cut-off the bike rider so that the car could proceed to make the right turn.

I'm sure we've all had situations of a car driver that wanted to demand the right-of-way and figured that a multi-ton car has more heft to decide the matter than does a fragile human on a bicycle.

What would an AI self-driving car do?

Right now, assuming that the AI sensors detected the bike rider, and assuming that the virtual world model was updated with the path of the bike rider, and assuming that the AI action planner portion of the system was able to anticipate a potential collision, presumably the AI would opt to brake and allow the bike rider to proceed.

We must also consider the traffic situation at the time, since we don't know what else might have been happening. Suppose a car was on the tail of the AI self-driving car and there was a risk that if the AI self-driving car abruptly halted, allowing the bike rider to proceed, the car behind the AI self-driving car might smack into the rear of the AI self-driving car. In that case, perhaps the risk of being hit from behind might lead the AI to determine that the risk of cutting off the bike rider is less overall and therefore proceed to cut-off the bike rider.

I mention this nuance about the AI self-driving car and its choice of what to do because of the oft times assumption by many that an AI self-driving car is always going to do "the right thing" in terms of making car driving decisions. In essence, people often tell me about situations of driving that they assume an AI system would "not make the same mistake" that a human made, and yet this assumption is often in a vacuum. Without knowing the context of the driving situation, how can we really say what the "right thing" was to do.

In any case, you might argue that the question brought up by the audience member is related to personalization and depersonalization. If the human driver was considering the human bike rider in a depersonalized way, they might have made the cut-off decision without any sense of humanity being involved.

Here's what might have been taking place. That's not a human on that bicycle, it is instead a thing on an object that is moving into my path and getting in my way of making that right turn, the driver might have been thinking. Furthermore, the driver might have been contemplating this: I am a human and my needs are important, and I need to make that right turn to proceed along smoothly and not be slowed down. The human driver objectifies the bike rider. The bike is an impediment. The human on the bike is meshed into the object.

Now, we don't know that's what the human driver was contemplating, but it is somewhat likely. It is easy when driving a car to fall into the mental trap that you are essentially in a video game. Around you are these various objects that are there to get in your way. Using your video gaming skills, you navigate in and around those objects.

If this seems farfetched, you might consider the emergence of road rage. People driving a car will at times become emboldened while in the driver's seat. They are in command of a vehicle that can determine life-or-death of others. This can inflate their sense of self-importance. They can become irked by other drivers and by pedestrians and decide to take this out on those around them.

As I've said many times in my speeches and in my writings, it is a miracle that we don't have more road rage than we already have. It is estimated that in the United States alone we drive a combined 3.22 trillion miles. Consider those 250 million cars in the United States and the drivers of those cars, and how unhinged some of them might be, or how unhinged they might become as a result of being slighted or they perceived they were slighted while driving, and it really is a miracle that we don't have more untoward driving acts.

Back to the bike rider that got cut-off, there is a possibility that the human driver depersonalized the bike rider. This once again illustrates that humans are not necessarily going to provide or undertake personalized acts in what they do.

An AI self-driving car might or might not be undertaking a more personalized approach, depending upon how the AI has been designed, developed, and fielded.

An AI self-driving car is going to encounter humans in a variety of ways. There will be human passengers inside the AI self-driving car. There will be pedestrians outside of the AI self-driving car and that the AI self-driving car comes across. There will be human drivers in other cars, of which the AI self-driving car will encounter while driving on the roadways. There will be human bike riders, along with other humans on motorcycles, scooters, and so on.

If you buy into the notion that the AI is by necessity a depersonalizing mechanism, meaning that in comparison to human drivers the AI driver will be acting toward humans in a depersonalized manner, more so than presumably other human drivers would, this seems to spell possible disaster for humans. Are all of these humans that might be encountered going to be treated as mere objects and not as humans?

The counter-argument is that the AI can be embodied with a form of personalization that would enhance the AI driver over the at-times depersonalizing human driver. The AI system might have a calculus that assesses the value of the bike as based on the human riding the bike. Unlike the human driver of earlier mention, presumably the AI is going to take into account that a human is riding the bike.

In the case of interacting with human passengers, there is a possibility of having the AI make use of sophisticated Natural Language Processing (NLP) and socio-behavioral conversational computing. In some ways, this could be done such that the personalization of interaction is on par with a typical human driver, perhaps even better so.

Take a look at Figure 2.

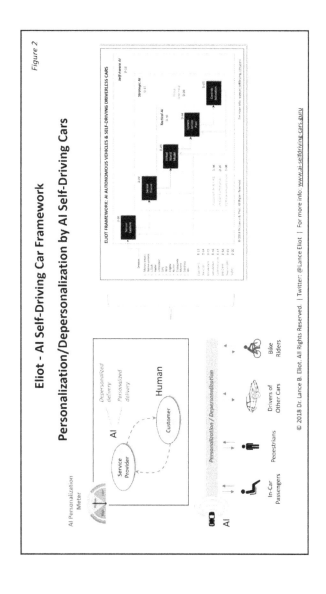

Have you been in a cab or taxi whereby the human driver was lacking in conversational ability, and unable to respond when you asked where's a good place to eat in this town? Or, the opposite extreme, you've been in a ridesharing car and the human driver was trying to be overly responsive by chattering the entire time, along with quizzing you about who you are, where you work, what you do. That's akin to my bank teller example earlier.

AI developers ought to be aiming for the Goldilocks version of interaction with human passengers. Not too little of conversation, and not too much. On some occasions, the human passenger will just want to say where they wish to go and not want any further discussion. In other cases, the human passenger might be seeking a vigorous dialogue. One size does not fit all.

In terms of interacting with humans that are outside of the AI self-driving car, there is definitely a bit of a problem on that end of things.

Just the other day, I drove up to a four-way stop. There was another car already stopped, sitting on the other side of the intersection, and apparently waiting. I wasn't sure why the other driver wasn't moving forward. They had the right-of-way. Were they worried that I wasn't going to come to a stop? Maybe they feared that I was going to run thru the stop signs and so they were waiting to make sure I came to a stop.

Well, after fully coming to a stop, I watched to see what the other car was going to do. Still no movement. I realize that most drivers in my shoes would zoom ahead, figuring that whatever the issue was about the other driver, it didn't matter. I was concerned that the other driver might suddenly lurch forward and maybe ram into me as I drove through the intersection. They were already doing something weird, and so in my mind they were prone to weirdness of driving action.

I rolled down my window and waved my arm at the other car, suggesting that they were free to move ahead. The other driver rolled down their window, popped their head out, and yelled something unintelligible (I was too far away to hear them), and proceeded to drive forward. After the car cleared the intersection, I also proceeded forward.

In this case, we humans communicated directly with each other, albeit somewhat imperfectly. I've described this in my writings and speeches as the "head nod" problem of AI self-driving cars.

How will an AI self-driving car communicate with humans that are outside of the car? They cannot nod their head or wave their arms, unless we decide to put robots into the driver's seat. Some auto maker and tech firms are outfitting the exterior of their AI self-driving cars with special screens or displays, allowing the AI to communicate via those means with humans outside of the self-driving car.

If an AI self-driving car has no means to do head nods or hand waving, it would likely be ascribed as depersonalizing that aspect of the driving act. The inclusion of special exterior screens or displays is an attempt to personalize the AI, making it seem less aloof and less non-human.

How far should we go in this? There are some concept cars that have large eyeball-like globes on the front of the self-driving car, and animated eyes that move back-and-forth, in the manner that a human eye glaze might move. Useful? Creepie? Time will tell.

Human car drivers are supposed to use their blinkers to signify their driving actions. AI self-driving cars also use blinkers. In that manner, they are the same.

Human drivers often use little micro-movements of the car, such as the tire positions and where they lean the car toward, in order to suggest driving actions that are imminent. We don't yet have AI self-driving cars mimicking this behavior, though I've predicted that we ought to and will do so.

Human drivers can try to make their car appear more conspicuous. This might include honking the horn. It can include turning your headlights on and off or using your high beams and then your low beams. These are all means by which the human driver can use to communicate with other humans. Likewise, the AI ought to be doing the same.

There is right now a dangerous timidity about most AI self-driving cars that makes them vulnerable to being pranked by humans. If you are a pedestrian and know that you can out-psych the AI by appearing to be moving from the curb to the street, getting the AI to bring the self-driving car to a halt mid-street, the odds are that we'll have lots of humans doing this. Critics of such actions by humans are saying we should outlaw those actions. Though outlawing it might be one means, I vote that we focus on making the AI good enough that it cannot get pranked, just as human drivers generally are not pranked.

Conclusion

I claim that depersonalization is not inevitable as the rise of more AI systems becomes prevalent.

If the AI systems are designed and developed such that they lack forms of personalization, I'd grant that we'll end-up with a lot of depersonalizing automated systems. The upside of using AI is that the chances of being able to embrace personalization is enhanced. Let's not squander that possibility.

AI self-driving cars are going to be one galvanizing lighting rod of qualms about depersonalization. For the design and development of AI self-driving cars, regrettably the personalization aspects are not especially yet being given their due by many of the auto makers and tech firms. The belief by some is that those are edge or corner cases, meaning that we can wait to deal with those aspects.

The first iterations of AI self-driving cars will likely determine the ongoing pace and acceptance of AI self-driving cars. We are setting ourselves up for a great deal of pushback if we delay or ignore the personalization factors. Those AI self-driving cars that seem to be depersonalizing will heighten the belief that they are not ready for prime time. Of course, that could be a correct assessment, namely that without proper personalization capabilities, maybe they shouldn't be on our roadways.

Human-to-human involves personalization and depersonalization. AI-to-human also involves personalization and depersonalization. AI developers would be wise to seek the personalization side of things and overcome or avoid the depersonalization side of things. That's what I personally say.

APPENDIX

APPENDIX A
TEACHING WITH THIS MATERIAL

The material in this book can be readily used either as a supplemental to other content for a class, or it can also be used as a core set of textbook material for a specialized class. Classes where this material is most likely used include any classes at the college or university level that want to augment the class by offering thought provoking and educational essays about AI and self-driving cars.

In particular, here are some aspects for class use:

o   Computer Science. Studying AI, autonomous vehicles, etc.

o   Business. Exploring technology and it adoption for business.

o   Sociology. Sociological views on the adoption and advancement of technology.

Specialized classes at the undergraduate and graduate level can also make use of this material.

For each chapter, consider whether you think the chapter provides material relevant to your course topic. There is plenty of opportunity to get the students thinking about the topic and force them to decide whether they agree or disagree with the points offered and positions taken. I would also encourage you to have the students do additional research beyond the chapter material presented (I provide next some suggested assignments they can do).

RESEARCH ASSIGNMENTS ON THESE TOPICS

Your students can find background material on these topics, doing so in various business and technical publications. I list below the top ranked AI related journals. For business publications, I would suggest the usual culprits such as the Harvard Business Review, Forbes, Fortune, WSJ, and the like.

Here are some suggestions of homework or projects that you could assign to students:

a) Assignment for foundational AI research topic: Research and prepare a paper and a presentation on a specific aspect of Deep AI, Machine Learning, ANN, etc. The paper should cite at least 3 reputable sources. Compare and contrast to what has been stated in this book.

b) Assignment for the Self-Driving Car topic: Research and prepare a paper and Self-Driving Cars. Cite at least 3 reputable sources and analyze the characterizations. Compare and contrast to what has been stated in this book.

c) Assignment for a Business topic: Research and prepare a paper and a presentation on businesses and advanced technology. What is hot, and what is not? Cite at least 3 reputable sources. Compare and contrast to the depictions in this book.

d) Assignment to do a Startup: Have the students prepare a paper about how they might startup a business in this realm. They must submit a sound Business Plan for the startup. They could also be asked to present their Business Plan and so should also have a presentation deck to coincide with it.

You can certainly adjust the aforementioned assignments to fit to your particular needs and the class structure. You'll notice that I ask for 3 reputable cited sources for the paper writing based assignments. I usually steer students toward "reputable" publications, since otherwise they will cite some oddball source that has no credentials other than that they happened to write something and post it onto the Internet. You can define "reputable" in whatever way you prefer, for example some faculty think Wikipedia is not reputable while others believe it is reputable and allow students to cite it.

The reason that I usually ask for at least 3 citations is that if the student only does one or two citations they usually settle on whatever they happened to find the fastest. By requiring three citations, it usually seems to force them to look around, explore, and end-up probably finding five or more, and then whittling it down to 3 that they will actually use.

I have not specified the length of their papers, and leave that to you to tell the students what you prefer. For each of those assignments, you could end-up with a short one to two pager, or you could do a dissertation length paper. Base the length on whatever best fits for your class, and the credit amount of the assignment within the context of the other grading metrics you'll be using for the class.

I mention in the assignments that they are to do a paper and prepare a presentation. I usually try to get students to present their work. This is a good practice for what they will do in the business world. Most of the time, they will be required to prepare an analysis and present it. If you don't have the class time or inclination to have the students present, then you can of course cut out the aspect of them putting together a presentation.

If you want to point students toward highly ranked journals in AI, here's a list of the top journals as reported by *various citation counts sources* (this list changes year to year):

o   Communications of the ACM

o   Artificial Intelligence

o   Cognitive Science

o   IEEE Transactions on Pattern Analysis and Machine Intelligence

o   Foundations and Trends in Machine Learning

o   Journal of Memory and Language

o   Cognitive Psychology

o   Neural Networks

o   IEEE Transactions on Neural Networks and Learning Systems

o   IEEE Intelligent Systems

o   Knowledge-based Systems

GUIDE TO USING THE CHAPTERS

For each of the chapters, I provide next some various ways to use the chapter material. You can assign the tasks as individual homework assignments, or the tasks can be used with team projects for the class. You can easily layout a series of assignments, such as indicating that the students are to do item "a" below for say Chapter 1, then "b" for the next chapter of the book, and so on.

a) What is the main point of the chapter and describe in your own words the significance of the topic,

b) Identify at least two aspects in the chapter that you agree with, and support your concurrence by providing at least one other outside researched item as support; make sure to explain your basis for disagreeing with the aspects,

c) Identify at least two aspects in the chapter that you disagree with, and support your disagreement by providing at least one other outside researched item as support; make sure to explain your basis for disagreeing with the aspects,

d) Find an aspect that was not covered in the chapter, doing so by conducting outside research, and then explain how that aspect ties into the chapter and what significance it brings to the topic,

e) Interview a specialist in industry about the topic of the chapter, collect from them their thoughts and opinions, and readdress the chapter by citing your source and how they compared and contrasted to the material,

f) Interview a relevant academic professor or researcher in a college or university about the topic of the chapter, collect from them their thoughts and opinions, and readdress the chapter by citing your source and how they compared and contrasted to the material,

g) Try to update a chapter by finding out the latest on the topic, and ascertain whether the issue or topic has now been solved or whether it is still being addressed, explain what you come up with.

The above are all ways in which you can get the students of your class involved in considering the material of a given chapter. You could mix things up by having one of those above assignments per each week, covering the chapters over the course of the semester or quarter.

As a reminder, here are the chapters of the book and you can select whichever chapters you find most valued for your particular class:

Companion Book By This Author

Advances in AI and Autonomous Vehicles:
Cybernetic Self-Driving Cars

Practical Advances in Artificial Intelligence (AI)
and Machine Learning
by
Dr. Lance B. Eliot, MBA, PhD

<u>Chapter Title</u>

This title is available via Amazon and other book sellers

Companion Book By This Author

Self-Driving Cars:
"The Mother of All AI Projects"

by Dr. Lance B. Eliot, MBA, PhD

This title is available via Amazon and other book sellers

Companion Book By This Author

*Innovation and Thought Leadership
on Self-Driving Driverless Cars*

by Dr. Lance B. Eliot, MBA, PhD

Chapter Title

This title is available via Amazon and other book sellers

<u>Companion Book By This Author</u>

New Advances in AI Autonomous Driverless Cars Self-Driving Cars

by Dr. Lance B. Eliot, MBA, PhD

<u>Chapter Title</u>

This title is available via Amazon and other book sellers

Companion Book By This Author

Introduction to
Driverless Self-Driving Cars

by Dr. Lance B. Eliot, MBA, PhD

Chapter Title

This title is available via Amazon and other book sellers

<u>Companion Book By This Author</u>

Autonomous Vehicle Driverless
Self-Driving Cars and Artificial Intelligence

by Dr. Lance B. Eliot, MBA, PhD

<u>Chapter Title</u>

This title is available via Amazon and other book sellers

Companion Book By This Author

Transformative Artificial Intelligence Driverless Self-Driving Cars

by Dr. Lance B. Eliot, MBA, PhD

This title is available via Amazon and other book sellers

Companion Book By This Author

Disruptive Artificial Intelligence and Driverless Self-Driving Cars

by Dr. Lance B. Eliot, MBA, PhD

This title is available via Amazon and other book sellers

Lance B. Eliot

Companion Book By This Author

State-of-the-Art
AI Driverless Self-Driving Cars

by Dr. Lance B. Eliot, MBA, PhD

<u>Chapter Title</u>

This title is available via Amazon and other book sellers

Companion Book By This Author

Top Trends in AI Self-Driving Cars

by Dr. Lance B. Eliot, MBA, PhD

Chapter Title

This title is available via Amazon and other book sellers

Companion Book By This Author

Crucial Advances for
AI Self-Driving Cars

by Dr. Lance B. Eliot, MBA, PhD

This title is available via Amazon and other book sellers

<u>Companion Book By This Author</u>

Sociotechnical Insights and AI Driverless Cars

by Dr. Lance B. Eliot, MBA, PhD

<u>Chapter Title</u>

This title is available via Amazon and other book sellers

Companion Book By This Author

Pioneering Advances for AI Driverless Cars

by Dr. Lance B. Eliot, MBA, PhD

This title is available via Amazon and other book sellers

Companion Book By This Author

Leading Edge Trends for
AI Driverless Cars

by Dr. Lance B. Eliot, MBA, PhD

Chapter Title

This title is available via Amazon and other book sellers

Companion Book By This Author

The Cutting Edge of
AI Autonomous Cars

by Dr. Lance B. Eliot, MBA, PhD

This title is available via Amazon and other book sellers

Companion Book By This Author

The Next Wave of AI Self-Driving Cars

by Dr. Lance B. Eliot, MBA, PhD

Chapter Title

This title is available via Amazon and other book sellers

<u>Companion Book By This Author</u>

Revolutionary Innovations of AI Self-Driving Cars

by Dr. Lance B. Eliot, MBA, PhD

<u>Chapter Title</u>

This title is available via Amazon and other book sellers

This title is available via Amazon and other book sellers

Companion Book By This Author

***Trailblazing Trends* for
AI Self-Driving Cars**

by Dr. Lance B. Eliot, MBA, PhD

This title is available via Amazon and other book sellers

Companion Book By This Author

Ingenious Strides for
AI Driverless Cars

by Dr. Lance B. Eliot, MBA, PhD

Chapter Title

1 Eliot Framework for AI Self-Driving Cars

2 Plasticity and AI Self-Driving Cars

3 NIMBY vs. YIMBY and AI Self-Driving Cars

4 Top Trends for 2019 and AI Self-Driving Cars

5 Rural Areas and AI Self-Driving Cars

6 Self-Imposed Constraints and AI Self-Driving Car

7 Alien Limb Syndrome and AI Self-Driving Cars

8 Jaywalking and AI Self-Driving Cars

This title is available via Amazon and other book sellers

Companion Book By This Author

AI Self-Driving Cars
Inventiveness

by Dr. Lance B. Eliot, MBA, PhD

Chapter Title

This title is available via Amazon and other book sellers

Companion Book By This Author

Visionary Secrets of AI Driverless Cars

by Dr. Lance B. Eliot, MBA, PhD

This title is available via Amazon and other book sellers

<u>Companion Book By This Author</u>

Spearheading
AI Self-Driving Cars

by Dr. Lance B. Eliot, MBA, PhD

<u>Chapter Title</u>

This title is available via Amazon and other book sellers

Lance B. Eliot

Companion Book By This Author

Spurring
AI Self-Driving Cars
by Dr. Lance B. Eliot, MBA, PhD

Chapter Title

This title is available via Amazon and other book sellers

Companion Book By This Author

Avant-Garde
AI Driverless Cars

by Dr. Lance B. Eliot, MBA, PhD

This title is available via Amazon and other book sellers

ABOUT THE AUTHOR

Dr. Lance B. Eliot, MBA, PhD is the CEO of Techbruim, Inc. and Executive Director of the Cybernetic AI Self-Driving Car Institute, and has over twenty years of industry experience including serving as a corporate officer in a billion dollar firm and was a partner in a major executive services firm. He is also a serial entrepreneur having founded, ran, and sold several high-tech related businesses. He previously hosted the popular radio show *Technotrends* that was also available on American Airlines flights via their in-flight audio program. Author or co-author of a dozen books and over 400 articles, he has made appearances on CNN, and has been a frequent speaker at industry conferences.

A former professor at the University of Southern California (USC), he founded and led an innovative research lab on Artificial Intelligence in Business. Known as the "AI Insider" his writings on AI advances and trends has been widely read and cited. He also previously served on the faculty of the University of California Los Angeles (UCLA), and was a visiting professor at other major universities. He was elected to the International Board of the Society for Information Management (SIM), a prestigious association of over 3,000 high-tech executives worldwide.

He has performed extensive community service, including serving as Senior Science Adviser to the Vice Chair of the Congressional Committee on Science & Technology. He has served on the Board of the OC Science & Engineering Fair (OCSEF), where he is also has been a Grand Sweepstakes judge, and likewise served as a judge for the Intel International SEF (ISEF). He served as the Vice Chair of the Association for Computing Machinery (ACM) Chapter, a prestigious association of computer scientists. Dr. Eliot has been a shark tank judge for the USC Mark Stevens Center for Innovation on start-up pitch competitions, and served as a mentor for several incubators and accelerators in Silicon Valley and Silicon Beach. He served on several Boards and Committees at USC, including having served on the Marshall Alumni Association (MAA) Board in Southern California.

Dr. Eliot holds a PhD from USC, MBA, and Bachelor's in Computer Science, and earned the CDP, CCP, CSP, CDE, and CISA certifications. Born and raised in Southern California, and having traveled and lived internationally, he enjoys scuba diving, surfing, and sailing.

ADDENDUM

Avant-Garde
AI Driverless Cars

Practical Advances in Artificial Intelligence (AI)
and Machine Learning

By
Dr. Lance B. Eliot, MBA, PhD

———

For supplemental materials of this book, visit:
www.ai-selfdriving-cars.guru

For special orders of this book, contact:
LBE Press Publishing
Email: LBE.Press.Publishing@gmail.com